Financial Security

Once
and
For All
and
Forever

How _Real_ Women Manage Wealth

Susan
Joyce

Financial Security Once and For All and Forever
How Real Women Manage Wealth

Published by
Women's Financial Focus Groups of Minnesota

This book is dedicated to all the women who've shared their fears and tears with me over the years. Your experiences were the hallmark of inspiration for this book and will serve as a guiding light to all of us as we create a new paradigm for the entire financial industry.

I wish to personally dedicate this book to my children:
Ty, Rachel, and Toby.
You are, have always been and always will be
the purpose of my life and the reason for everything I do.

Women's Financial Focus Groups of Minnesota™

is a registered trademark in the State of Minnesota.

Women's Financial Focus Groups of Minnesota provides

education on wealth management to

women, men, couples, and teens.

ACKNOWLEDGEMENTS

This book would never have been written had it not been for the interest of Amy Stilwell, a fellow financial advisor, who ignited the firestorm which consumed my life for three years, Annie Meehan, motivational speaker and author, whose words and encouragement kept me focused, and Cheryl Leitschuh, life coach and author, for teaching me how to set goals and attain them. However, the artesian well of inspiration bubbled forth from all the women in my life who've intentionally and unintentionally exposed their vulnerabilities with regard to wealth management. While I regret the perilous situations that these women were subjected to I am grateful for the passion it stirred within me that compelled me to write this book.

Extreme gratitude to the amazing women in my life who not only sat for hours and hours listening to me prattle on and on, but who contributed valuable insight about the hearts and minds of women everywhere that led to the format for both the book and the supporting articles: Deb Oscarson, Cherri Martinek, Arlene Hueman, Karen Harrington, Jodi Johnson, April Gorton, Vergie Asper, Joan Anderson, Sue Jorgenson, and most of all Nancy Lauermann who withstood the most prattling and boldly went where others feared to go. Your support was integral and I cherish your friendship.

I would not be who I am today without the influence of the women in my family: Muriel Sheets, Louise Gardner (deceased), Betty Wood (deceased), Elaine Miller, Rachel Schommer, Lori Schommer, Jennifer Schommer; and I would be amiss to not admit that I pray this book benefits my granddaughters: Rebekka, Naimy, Adeline, Hannah, and Maggie, as well as my grandsons who support the women in their lives: Alhrik, Gannon, Jacob, and Lucas; and to all the women in my life who I consider as sisters: Arlene, Julie, Rita, Marcia, Karen, Judy, Joyce, Pat, Ardy, Nancy, Jackie F. (deceased), Barb (deceased), Ila, Mary, Jill, Dianna, Marsha, and Jackie K . – you are an indelible part of my heart.

Held in high esteem are the Park Avenue Authors: Georgia Whitmore (pen name: Claudia Ryan Smith), Neil Opstad, Jodi Johnson (pen name: J. L. Waldemar), April Gorton, Jim Troe, Sara Aeikens, Joyce

Nixon, Milt Ost, Hannah Schommer, Meridee Strouf, Elton Mertes, Dori Ethridge, Becky Goodell and Rachel Thompson – you are my sustenance. May my comradery be as valuable to you as yours is to me.

Special appreciation to author, editor and my mentor Mike Kalmbach – the master of tact and poignancy. Mike turned grueling tasks into insightful experiences, was the calm within my personal storm, my oasis in foreign and uncharted territory, and allowed me to write with abandon knowing he could handle everything that spilled out of my head and into my manuscript.

Much appreciation for the expedience and availability of David W. Koehser, attorney at law, who protected me from myself as well as from the ills of this world.

I owe a debt of gratitude to my husband, Dr. Steven J. Carlson, who really knows how to live with an author. Thank you for all the breakfasts at my desk and all the whine and wine dinners, and for being the sounding board to the entire text as well as all my bright and not-so-bright ideas. The path would not have been nearly as straight without your input.

And last, but not least, I am blessed by two little rescue dogs, Taffy and Tuffy who kept me consistently humbled to the realities as well as the joys of life. It is time for a nice long walk.

Table of Contents

Liability limit and disclaimer of warranty

The author, publisher, distributor, and any other person affiliated with the writing, publishing or distribution of this book make no representations or warranties with respect to the accuracy, completeness or currency of the contents of this book. The information conveyed in this book is not meant to be and should not be relied upon as advice or recommendations. The author, publisher, distributor and any person affiliated with this book disclaim any implied warranties of merchantability or fitness for any particular purpose, and specifically disclaim any damage, liability, or loss incurred, directly or indirectly, from the use or application of any of the contents of this book, including, without limitation, any special, incidental, consequential, or other damages.

This book is intended for educational purposes, to offer general information on how to acquire financial advice in the current market place within the United States. It is not intended to provide any specific investment advice or recommend or endorse any particular investment practices, products or advisors. Readers are responsible for reviewing their own financial situation, determining their own financial goals, and selecting suitable practices, strategies, products and advisors to assist them in achieving those goals.

TRADEMARKS: All brand names and product names used in this book are trade names, service marks, trademarks, or registered trademarks of their respective owners and are used only to identify the products or services of those owners. The Women's Financial Focus Groups of Minnesota is not associated with any product, service or vendor mentioned in this book and does not endorse the products or services of any vendor mentioned in this book.

Except for the website associated with this work, the author, publisher and others associated with the publication and distribution of this book are not affiliated with and do not sponsor or endorse any websites, organizations or other sources of information referred to herein, or warrant the accuracy, completeness or currency of any information or recommendations provided by those sources.

Preface

As a financial advisor with a major Wall Street firm, I witnessed far too many women in situations that could have been avoided if they had just a little information and a dose of self-confidence. All throughout my tenure as a financial advisor I witnessed reluctance in women verses men to engage in active wealth management. Even when prompted by their spouses, women still seemed reticent to contribute toward making important decisions about their wealth, leaving matters to their spouse, a son, their father or some other male in their life, or me (their financial advisor).

This is exactly what a woman should never, ever, *ever* do. So why do women do it? That became my quest.

I didn't find viable answers until I was afforded a unique opportunity to research the differences between the genders relative to financial decisions. That's when everything suddenly made sense.

Once I realized what had been overlooked for so long, I was able to develop a wealth management program just for women. This book is meant to:

- open everyone's eyes to what women really need
- offer women an immediate method to navigate effectively in the current male-oriented financial environment
- eradicate myths that prevent women from taking full control of their wealth
- provide women with the direction they need to fully utilize all their resources to fulfill their every desire

Financial Security
Once and **For All** and **Forever**
How *Real* Women Manage Wealth

The following articles support the topics found in this book in more detail and are available for purchase at:

www.RealWomenManageWealth.com

Article # 1 How Real Women Get What They Want
Identify what you really want out of life.

Article # 2 How Real Women Adapt Gender Differences
Recognize the power and limitations of being a woman.

Article # 3 How Real Women Guard Against Sales Tactics
Protect yourself from people capitalizing on your vulnerabilities.

Article # 4 How Real Women Vote
Understand the impact government has on your personal wealth.

Article # 5 How Real Women Treat Tax Laws
Maximize tax advantages for every stage of life.

Article # 6 How Real Women Utilize Bank Products
Fully utilize bank products and services.

Article # 7 How Real Women Buy Insurance
Effectively use insurance products as a wealth management tools.

Article # 8 How Real Women Shop for Investment Advice
Get what you need without giving them more than you should.

Article # 9 How Real Women Lay Down Their Own Law
Incorporate legal services efficiently and effectively.

Article # 10 How Real Women Change the World of Finance
Demand what you need from the financial industry.

Introduction

Women are natural-born wealth managers. They, not investors, are the leading force behind the global economy, yet the entire financial world (banking, insurance, investments, taxes, and law) continues to ignore this market segment. As a result, women are deprived of essential products and services needed to manage one of their greatest resources – money. Most women assume that the current financial world is as good as it gets, which exacerbates the negative impact that the financial industry has on them. Instead, women need to demand something different.

The current financial environment often makes women feel unqualified to manage their own money, but nothing could be farther from the truth. Women instinctively understand markets and are intuitive to a degree that can't yet be comprehended fully by the scientific community, but has now been recognized as legitimate by neuroscientists.

Studies prove women are more apt at sound wealth management than males, but the female market has been excluded by the financial industry largely due to social expectations and norms. As a result, women often find wealth management difficult, confusing and/or boring because everything about the financial industry was created *by* males *for* males.

As females outlive males, the world of finance is in the beginning of an inevitable renaissance. Females have already become the major wealth holders in the United States, but while the financial industry is licking their lips at this burgeoning new market, just ask any female consumer if she enjoys managing money and you will get the same old yawn.

The reason? Gender differences. Women shop, compare, and analyze differently than men before making a decision. Yet financial products are created and marketed the same old way: targeting only males. Women, however, have the power to change an entire industry by recognizing their own needs and demanding what they want from an industry that, for all intents and purposes, wants to give it to them. Until the entire financial market becomes more attractive to females and offers more suitable products and services geared toward the needs of *REAL* women, however, women will remain underserved by an entire financial industry which guides the use of the world's most powerful resource – money. The same old financial service models and products no more meet the needs of women than jock straps. The opposite sex is opposite in more ways than one.

All the financial courses and all the books on financial management in the world cannot prepare anyone to adequately manage their own wealth for one key reason: without the proper credentials, training and experience in all five areas of wealth management (banking, insurance, investments, taxes and law) one lacks the necessary expertise and objectivity. This book does not profess to teach you how to do everything yourself, but rather how to get the experts to do what they do best while you oversee everything they do. This method is the only way to minimize error and maximize the power of your wealth for your own purposes (and no one else's). While this method benefits both genders, it requires following directions, and therein may be the reason it hasn't been available up until now.

To lead a fulfilling life, funnel your time, talents and money toward the things most important to you.

CHAPTER 1:
You already know
everything you need to know.

To manage wealth effectively, you don't need to be an expert in banking, insurance, investments, taxes or law. In fact, the less you know about those things the better off you will be. What you need to know, however, is how to determine the type of professional advice you need at the time you need it and how to qualify it properly. This is where most people get into trouble and where women are the most vulnerable.

Neuroscience and statistics now prove that women not only are good wealth managers, but they outperform their male counterparts. This despite the fact they do not have suitable products, services and/or tools with which to do so.

Women today hold more than 60% of the wealth in the USA and by 2020 will hold even a greater portion. Women are today's primary prospects for the entire financial industry: banking, insurance, investments, taxes and law. But little has changed in the financial industry to adequately meet the needs of women. Women, themselves, do not yet know what is missing, but one thing is clear – women are not representing themselves equally according to the statistics. Women take a far less active role in wealth management than men even though they have greater influence over household spending. Women determine everything from which soup and nuts to buy to what the thermostat setting ought to be which drives markets all around the world from toys to oil.

If women were ever to participate equal to their counterparts in all five areas of finance, there is no telling how it could affect their lives, as well as the world. Wall Street market analysts chase statistics and anxiously watch leading economic indicators while pouring over past performances of a litany of companies in a myriad of industries, but they overlook the most powerful factor – women. Women are the leading indicator in every single market from energy to retail. Women are the driving-force behind retail and manufacturing largely because women make 80% of household purchase decisions. Analysts and economists all over the world track consumer spending using hindsight rather than foresight. If women just became more aware of their own behavior they would have the edge when it comes to anticipating market movements. Women already know what the economists are trying to understand. They just need to know how to properly use that information to their own advantage.

Take for instance the fast food industry. In 1950, one in three women were employed outside the home, or 33.9%. By 1998, three in five women were employed outside the home, or 59.8%. With more than half of all women in the workforce, is it any wonder why fast food chains sprang up all over the country? Anyone juggling child-rearing, household chores, and a job all at the same time can understand the need for fast food. Only market analysts were foolish enough to believe it was because the food tasted so good.

One car in every garage during the 50s turned into two cars in every driveway by the 70s. Detroit believed it was because of their advertising campaigns, but it was actually the first wave of female Baby-Boomers who were just graduating high school with different aspirations than their mothers who changed that landscape. The different values between the Boomers and Millennials, between the Millennials and Gen-Xers, and so on and so forth predict economic trends. Who better knows them than women?

The failure of U.S. automakers to recognize the emergence of the female market was overlooked and misanalysed. While Detroit was still appealing to male egos in the 80s offering big, powerful automobiles, females were drawn to foreign automobiles which provided practicality during a period of time in their lives where paying daycare and buying school supplies was a greater priority than buying gas. Imagine how this foresight could have impacted investment portfolios, not to mention the entire town of Detroit.

For many reasons, from the lack of male support to new female attitudes, the deterioration of the institution of marriage brought about another economic impact by the 1980s. Joint custody requires twice as many toys, bicycles, toothbrushes and beds as the number of children. Durable goods, as well as discretionary spending, increased for logical reasons which market analysts overlooked while any divorced mother could have predicted.

Today more than 6 in 10 women work outside the home. Any guesses as to what is about to happen? If you really want to know, ask a Baby-Boomer female who is planning her retirement. My bet would be on anything which might attract the interest of a new grandmother or an aging woman as she outlives her male counterparts. That might mean a surge in travel services, toys, eyewear and pharmaceuticals. Consider the type of car she might drive, or not drive. Ask a Gen-Xer who has been a stay-at-home mom what she plans to do when her children are all school age. If she returns to the workforce she will need a new wardrobe and transportation. That might mean a surge in retail fashion, but with the advent of light rail and other transportation services maybe it won't affect auto manufacturing as it once did when her grandmother went to work, or maybe it will. If you want to know which way the wind might blow ask a Gen-Xer. Ask a Millennial what she plans to do after college. I haven't a clue, but you can bet these women will know more quickly than any analyst armed only with hindsight. Women are a leading indicator of both national and world economics and a powerhouse of knowledge about themselves and other women in their lives.

Does it not make sense to ask women what they intend to buy tomorrow, or five years from now, or what they would like to buy if it were available?

While economic forecasts are a little more complicated, the point is women are being overlooked. And the point of this book is to show women how to take advantage of the power within themselves instead of waiting around to be noticed.

While the female market is hideously underserved by the financial community, women must share some of the blame. The financial industry must make a profit to remain competitive in business. The object of the financial industry is to minimize time spent at the point-of-sale as a means to maximize profits. As much as I hate to say this, it takes less time and energy to sell to a male than it does a female. Women discourage being prospected by financial professionals largely because they drag out a buying decision beyond the tolerance of most salespeople. While financial firms promote marketing to women, their sales force remains reluctant. I don't have a solution for this. The solution lies with women themselves, as they are the only ones who can determine how to become more viable prospects while at the same time protecting their rights to individualized services and products. It is a conundrum at the present time, but I believe women hold the answers.

Another thing women already understand to their advantage is wealth management is complicated. You don't need to convince them that any sort of investment is serious business. Just because males tend to ignore this fact is no reason women should. To manage wealth effectively and efficiently one needs to respect the risks as well as identify the reasons to take it. Women are naturally risk perverse. They have built-in barometers which, if correctly interpreted, could guide all their financial decisions more aptly than any current quantitative strategy used by professionals today.

Because sound wealth management coordinates all five areas of finance suitably to every situation, knowing how to do that is your only assurance that you are making the best decision about one of your most valuable resources – your money. If you leave your financial decisions up to a male, you are less likely to get a result that is comprehensive relative to your needs. You will learn how to rely on your instincts by the end of this book, but right now it is important for you to realize the significance of knowing what you already know.

Women are more suitable to sound wealth management than men because they are less encumbered by what they *think* they know, are more competent at shopping and comparing, and tend to follow directions better than their counterparts – all of which are attributes of sound wealth management. By their very nature, women are less egotistical than males and are less likely to pretend they know more than they do. This attribute initiates more productive investigations that lead to better decisions.

It is foolish to try and become an expert at everything, especially at something which changes rapidly moment by moment and encompasses the buying decisions of every living person on Earth. Banking, insurance, investments, taxes and law are all part of wealth management and must be coordinated for any one of these areas to work effectively. Therefore, you'd have to be an expert in all five areas before you could sufficiently manage your wealth without the help of experts in those fields.

Herein lies the conundrum: while you need expert advice, you must never accept it blindly. This is where women fail most often. They rely too heavily on the advice they obtain from experts, or on the advice of males they know and trust, such as their fathers, husbands, and/or sons. The funny thing is, it should be the other way around. Two thousand and fifty years of suppression will do that to a person. Women have been prevented from controlling world wealth since Cleopatra – one of the foremost wealth managers of all time. Today women possess a greater portion of the world's wealth than ever before. It is high time women resume their role as wealth managers, at least for themselves.

*Women have been
financially suppressed
for over two thousand years.*

Before making decisions about your money, you need to be enlightened to the wiles of the entire financial industry and be well-prepared to maneuver within it suitably to *your* specific needs – not theirs. Those wiles are the very reasons the financial industry is so heavily regulated. However, there are not enough eyes to watch over everyone trying to make a buck on your buck, so you need to be vigilant. It is impossible to protect yourself from any financial advisor (banker, insurance agent, investment advisor, tax advisor, lawyer) unless you are able to identify poor advice when you hear it. Maneuvering effectively between and within the five areas of financial services is essential to sound wealth management, but few people, males included, know how to do it. By the time you finish this book you will know how to acquire professional advice in all five areas of finance, how to apply that advice effectively, and how to avoid paying anyone a fee or commission for advice that isn't worth a dime. For now, just absorb this new vantage point over an old subject as I show you how.

The important thing to realize at this point is you do not need to know anything about banking, insurance, investments, taxes, or law. The only thing you need to be an expert on is yourself. You need to know what you want and when you want it. That's it. That's all there is to managing your wealth suitably to your desires. Therefore, you already know everything you need to know. Learn to convey your personal objectives to financial professionals and let them explain how their products and/or services will help you achieve whatever it is you wish to accomplish. Just don't fall for their sales pitch, but rather use the method outlined in this book.

Most women feel anxious about having to make important decisions about wealth, and that is because the financial world has almost exclusively marketed to males, thus far. Imagine the anxiety women felt when the fashion industry began marketing trousers for women in place of bustles. While you may be ready to wear the pants, the only thing available is bustles at the moment. However, no one needs to be an Annie Oakley to function well within a male-oriented environment. What you *will* need, however, is a clear target and a hired gun (figuratively speaking, of course), or in this case a financial expert. So, start with knowing why you need money, when you will need it, and how much you will need. This is your target. Gunslingers only aim at what they are told to hit. Same with financial advisors. If you are unable to tell them exactly what you want to achieve, they will aim at the easiest target. Therefore, it is imperative that you advise your advisors correctly, so you must understand what you want, when you want it and how much it will cost.

Any expert in one of the five areas of finance is unqualified to offer advice in any other area. Try to avoid assuming that you are getting good wealth management advice from any one financial expert (banker, insurance agent, investment advisor, tax advisor, or lawyer). When you go to any one of these experts, you are only getting limited suggestions as to what their particular firm or area of expertise offers. However, you need to know all the options from all five areas before you can make a good decision as to what is best for you and your particular situation. If one knows the process of acquiring the right type of advice at the right time, anyone is as qualified as the next to manage their own wealth. Here again, lies the biggest challenge. Knowing who to go to, for what, and when. But the answer is easy: go to them all! Shop.

If you are able to articulate what you want, you have all the qualifications necessary to effectively manage your wealth. You just need to know how to utilize what you already know effectively. Well...there is just one tiny other thing you need to do. Forget everything you think you already know about managing wealth, and prepare your mind to embrace a new way of thinking. The concepts you will discover in this book are part of a revelation that is just beginning to emerge within our society. I am not the only one out here trying to help women by introducing a female-friendlier concept of wealth management. I am just the one who caught *your* attention. This is only the beginning.

You've been led to believe things that are not in your best interests. It is time we do away with such myths and recognize the facts.

MYTH: Married couples/life partners should share a common financial plan to save money and to avoid overlap.

FACT: Nothing could be farther from the truth. Sharing the same financial plan is no different than sharing the same exact wardrobe. While there may be things you could share, there are bound to be significant personal differences.

MYTH: Married couples/life partners should use the same financial advisor(s) for advice.

FACT: One cannot serve two masters at the same time and be fair to both.

MYTH: Financial professionals, such as estate attorneys, certified public accountant, insurance agents, and investment advisors, offer financial advice suitable to both men and women that can always be trusted.

FACT: The entire financial industry does not yet know what women need, therefore, it is impossible for any financial expert to offer services or products suitable to women. Besides, all financial professionals are selling something. Their advice is not offered as a public service, but rather as a sales pitch.

MYTH: People who love us won't take advantage of us.

FACT: Really? Think about it.

MYTH: We should never rely on our intuition or 'gut feeling' when it comes to wealth management.

FACT: Women's intuition works something like a computer when it calculates a bazillion bits of information in a nanosecond to produce a likely conclusion, or answer. It is so highly complicated neuroscience has yet to define it, but the scientific community recognizes it as a viable entity. Never discount a woman's intuition any more than you'd discount any aspect of nature.

MYTH: Men are naturally better wealth managers than women.

FACT: Women consistently outperform males in all matters of finance from better debt control to higher rates of return on investments.

MYTH: If you didn't earn the money yourself, you have no right managing it because it isn't yours.

FACT: Legally married partners share all assets under the law, including income, inheritance, and debt. Exercise your rights.

Women do two things which undermine themselves. One, they tend to share their wealth more freely with others, particularly males in their lives: spouses, lovers, family members, friends, and even strangers. Two, they fail to identify their own value. More women than men fail to consider their legal rights to household income, and women more so than men fail to calculate the value of employee benefits and negotiate such to their advantage prior to accepting employment.

If you leave the management of your wealth up to anyone else, you will be giving that person rights to manage it according to *their* needs over your own. That includes commission, fees, or just plain buying whatever they want with your money.

Sound wealth management is personal to your individual needs and desires.

Sound wealth management is a process of acquiring information about the options available to you prior to making a decision. Gender-specific tendencies provide women all the necessary attributes without having to acquire one bit of education about any of the five areas of finance: banking, insurance, investments, taxes and law, so long as you use professionals in each of these areas correctly. Women have the greatest capacity for managing wealth for themselves and their households and already know everything else they need to know.

CHAPTER 2:

It's time women take the whole cake.

The roles and challenges women face today are vastly different than those of their mothers and grandmothers. Within just the past two decades, women's lives have changed dramatically. Divorce, widowhood, social security, pensions, financial services and education, even politics all present vastly different challenges for women than men.

- More than 7 out of 10 women still prefer to delegate financial matters to someone else, even an advisor, than to handle it themselves;
- Barely 2 out of every 10 women have calculated their retirement needs;
- Yet 9 out of 10 women classify retirement planning as their MOST important issue.

As a woman you should expect to spend more time taking care of your own financial matters for a longer period of time, with fewer resources than your spouse – or men in general.

Things have changed
since your mother's time.

Why won't the same wealth management tactics work as well for women as men? Why do women need different advice, service and/or products than men? For a lot of reasons.

For one, women in the workforce continue to face obstacles while trying to achieve their professional goals.

- They make lower wages, $0.78 to the dollar.
- They pay emotional and financial consequences as a result of putting others first while holding down a job: child rearing, taking care of aging parents, etc.
- Domestic violence: women make up the majority of reported domestic violence victims – as a result: 96% of victims experience problems at work, 74% are harassed while at work by their abuser; and as a result 56% are late to work; 28% leave work early; and 54% miss entire days of work as a result of problems at home.

Employers lose between $3-$5billion dollars every year to issues surrounding domestic violence.

Beyond domestic violence, women spend less time in the workforce than men, due also to child-rearing and taking care of aging parents. Women continue to dominate child-rearing duties and responsibilities, which limits their time in the workforce or in some cases, even eliminates it for a period of years. Many couples mutually agree about the benefits of one parent staying home during adolescent years, but if women don't work outside the home, they do not build any social security or pension benefits for themselves.

They are vulnerable to whatever their husbands provide. I remind you 51% of all marriages fail, and of the remainder many of these wives are not living in bliss.

Up until 1867 divorces were so rare they were not even recorded. The marriage failure rate was low largely because of social stigma and the lack of economic opportunities for women outside marriage were nil at the time. It was not on account women were more happily married. They just had fewer options.

Between 1867-1879 it was reported that 3% of marriages failed. By 1900 that figure jumped to 7% and has increased ever since. By 1966 the divorce rate was at 25%. By 1980 you had less than a 50/50 chance of a happy marriage – the divorce rate was 52% and rising...need I say more?

Divorce continues to pose additional burdens on women versus men, such as stigma, social implications, and self-esteem.

After divorce women's egos tend to deteriorate, while men's egos tend to inflate.

Some of the reasons women experience added burdens after a divorce is because more often they have primary custody of the children – now without the help of a spouse, in addition to being responsible for all household chores and maintenance. In top of that they are far more likely than males to become skeptical of marriage or long-term partnerships – which impose self-limits which ultimately eliminates a woman's legal rights to additional household income and benefits.

Women pay a consequence for their values. According to the Family Caregiver Alliance, 66% of women take on the role of primary caregiver or underaged children. This makes women less likely than men to be able to retire at age 65 due to lost income and benefits. More than 5 out of 10 women plan to retire after the age of 65 or not at all, according to the Transamerica Center for Retirement Studies. That's half of all women who are not financially able to retire according to current statistics.

- Women live longer than men.
  - They need more money to cover living expenses
  - They need more money for healthcare.
    - A woman at age 65 needs $86,000 to have a 50% chance of being able to pay for all future healthcare costs, whereas a man needs a minimum of $65,000 at the same age.
    - A woman's financial plan needs to include $139,000 to cover healthcare costs.
    - A man's financial plan needs $122,000.

Let's see…women get paid less, have to do more, and need more money than a man to live the same life. What is wrong with this picture? And who is really helping her understand her situation, and will help her do something about it? Statistics don't lie…so we know it is NOT the men in this world. A man cannot possibly understand what a woman faces, no matter how sensitive he is or how much he wants to understand. Men just don't get it and they never will.

The world needs you. You need to figure out what you need, how you need it, and how you want to get it, then communicate your needs to all financial professionals until they hear you and answer you appropriately. Like the Founding Fathers of our nation, you will become the Founding Mothers of a new way to manage wealth and will set the example for others to follow. You have just begun your adventure as a wealth manager.

Women outlive men. The average age of widowhood is 56 in this country. Between women living longer in retirement than men, women needing more money to fulfill their life expectancy, and the fact they have fewer options to avoid economic hardship than men, every woman should be concerned.

Widowhood puts women at great risk for economic hardship and the situation declines with duration.

Household income declines when either spouse dies, but for women it often declines far more than for men. Before ERISA and the Retirement Equity Act, men were allowed to choose a single-life payout of their pension without their wives ever knowing. That meant they got more money while they were alive, and their wives got nothing when they died. Wives were at the mercy of their husbands, and the evidence was that men were not very merciful. Thus a law was enacted to protect women: The *Employee Retirement Income Security Act (ERISA) of 1974 changed a single life payout to a joint-and-survivor benefit.*

The *Retirement Equity Act (REA) of 1984* offered women additional consideration. It amended ERISA to require the spouse's signature if a worker wants to select the single-life benefit. The result substantially affected the number of widows who receive a survivor pension.

While total loss of pension benefits after the working spouse's death has become uncommon, full retention is still rare. Therefore, it is essential that you know and understand how you will be affected by financial decisions your spouse makes and represent your own interests effectively in any relationship in which you are involved.

Something more about PENSIONS –

- Women work in areas where pensions are not as likely to be offered as the areas in which men work, therefore, women have far fewer pension benefits as a whole.
- Women still need to learn to identify pensions and other benefits and evaluate them as they do wages. This is one of those areas in which women have been left in the dust by men in our society. How many conversations with other women have you had about pension benefits? If negotiated correctly, employee benefits can double a person's wages.

Another matter women should be concerned about is Social Security. When a spouse dies and both are receiving Social Security, the surviving spouse can choose the larger of the two benefits, but the other benefit ceases forever. If the only income is Social Security, household income can decline by as much as half. Since women outlive men, this is more likely to happen to you than your spouse.

Income ceases altogether if your spouse was still earning a wage, not to mention his social security contributions cease – thereby affecting your future as well as your immediate circumstance.

Women have minimal options to improve their economic situation after widowhood or divorce.

- Women earn $.78 on the dollar to a man's wages if she chooses to continue to work, or go into the workforce after widowhood. Because she earns less, she earns less in Social Security benefits, not to mention all the other benefits which are based on her lower wages:
  - Company contributions to retirement plans
  - Pension benefits
  - Profit sharing
  - Unemployment benefits
  - Worker's Compensation
- Earning income becomes more difficult with age for both genders, but while men are more physically apt and able to perform the majority of the same duties women can perform, many women cannot fulfill the same physical requirements as a man. Women, therefore, have fewer employment options as they age.
- Remarriage is an option, but you could give up all potential benefits left by your deceased husband if you choose to remarry – statistically remarriages are not any more certain than any other marriage. If you remarry, you are entitled to *that* spouse's Social Security benefits if you remain married to him for at least 10 years, but you could give up rights to your former spouse's benefits. While love is blind, don't you be.
- Living with children or relatives reduces a woman's independence and affects her self-image and self-esteem.

The stability of the Social Security entitlement is a whole different matter for women than it is for men.

Social Security will begin to run out in 2034 and is anticipated to pay only $0.76 on the dollar. No matter if you believe Social Security will be there for you by the time you retire, or whether our government will come up with another way of securing social positions for us citizens – you can bet the situation for women won't change much. Women should be more concerned than men about the preservation of social status largely because women, as a whole, are more vulnerable to poverty after divorce and widowhood. Women are heavily reliant on Social Security benefits because of wage and employment discrimination and different patterns of labor force participation.

Despite changes in women's workforce participation, there are social patterns that still persist. Survivor benefits are less than a spouse's benefit, and this on top of the fact a widow can only collect one Social Security benefit.

While life might seem unfair, the Social Security program here in the United States values women and children as homemakers and as mothers of the next generation of tax-payers. Since women are more vulnerable than men, Social Security benefits become far more important to women. Social Security benefits are safe, reliable, and guaranteed for life, unlike private investments which can devalue and unlike pension funds which sometimes can blow up and go away due to bankruptcy and defaults. Social Security benefits have cost-of-living increases built into it, which is good for women since they live longer than men and need more protection against inflation. Social Security recognizes the value of women as homemakers and widows with children and provides benefits to women in the absence of any other protection for women. While far from perfect, Social Security is the most stable financial source for women as a whole.

Our government, as much as it represents the interests of all citizens and tries to do so equally, does not equally represent the needs of females compared to males.

In 1935 Social Security provided that only 3.5% of total wages could be paid to the estate of a worker in certain cases. Lump-sum benefits were insufficient for widows, so Congress enacted changes in 1939.

- Congress added new types of widow benefits for disabled widows and modified the two original types of benefits.
- Divorced spouses no longer lose their benefits.

Today, if your husband is self-employed and does not pay into social security, you have no benefits unless you work outside the home and pay into Social Security yourself. Many women who stay at home do not realize this and are blindsided at retirement.

Child-in-care widows often have benefits reduced because of Social Security family maximum provisions. If you are widowed while you still have dependent children, you are entitled to benefits, but once the kids grow up and you become eligible for retirement benefits, those benefits will be reduced because of maximums placed on benefits you've already received. Don't be blindsided by your own decisions.

Our government system is created to represent the majority. Women already outnumber men and in the future will significantly outnumber men. If we are the majority, then our concerns should be at the forefront of our government. Stand up for yourself in politics. The vote you cast should benefit you and only you. Encourage other women to represent their needs, and our system will truly meet the needs of the majority in the way it was meant to do.

Don't vote as your spouse does just to avoid cancelling his vote. Consider he could be cancelling yours.

Political issues are paramount to women, yet often are ignored by them. In 1974 and again in 1984, when widows fell into poverty in record numbers, it was the federal government which discovered the reason and put in place measures to prevent others from falling to the same fate. Apparently pension benefit recipients (mostly men) were taking everything for themselves while leaving nothing to their spouses once they died.

Now it is a requirement that a wife sign-off before her husband chooses an option which might leave her high and dry. The Senate Finance Committee, however, continues to report concerns about widows with too little overall income. Be sure you know which candidate in your voting district has your best interests at heart. As a female, your financial security is at greater risk than a male's. Know what your government is and isn't doing to protect your rights and support the party and candidates who best represent your interests. Your own personal needs should dictate which way you vote. The way in which you vote affects your overall financial situation, therefore, politics and voting effectively is part of sound wealth management.

CHAPTER 3:
He's never going to change, and neither will you.

Neuroscience now has proof that the Corpus Callosum is different in men and women. Men have four percent more brain cells than women, but a woman's brain is four times more active than man's. Women process information from one side of the brain to the other four times more often, and do it faster than men.

Instead of risking that I might bore you to death and lose your interest altogether by subjecting you to all the scientific facts which support gender differences, I am going to risk that I might offend you by stereotyping men and women so we can both get through this book without caffeine. Let me make my apologies in advance and warn you that the following pages include content meant only for mature minds.

How do differences between the genders affect wealth management? Women can do everything men do, so what is the point?

Men created the financial industry. Therefore, everything about it appeals to the male psyche. Males prefer less stimuli and tend to focus on one thing at a time, while women require a multitude of stimuli before they can narrow their focus to one thing. The financial industry was made to appeal to men, not women. It is one-on-one, singular in product offering, and the environment is not conducive for any other purpose but for doing business the way men prefer to do business.

Conversely, shopping malls were created to appeal to women, not men. While each gender functions in both environments, they excel in certain environments. When it comes to managing your money, you want an environment, products and services which prompt your *best* decisions. That can only happen in an environment which meets the needs of your particular gender, but that isn't the case at the moment. Women are in male territory whenever they seek products or services of a bank, insurance company, investment firm, tax firm or law office.

Even if you are one who can effectively play by the boys' rules, it would be wise to realize that the female culture does not offer as many financial opportunities to women as the male culture offers men. Everything from casual discussions to actual investment opportunities is rampant in the male culture, while not so much among females. At the risk of stereotyping, it would be like suggesting that the majority of men have been equally exposed to matters of childcare as have females. Just merely by being a woman, you've been exposed to more information, role-models, and influence regarding child-rearing than your male counterparts.

Gender differences exist. One gender isn't better than the other. There are just differences between the genders which need to be respected and understood if you want to manage your wealth appropriately. The male and female cultures are strong whether a person is typical or atypical. It doesn't matter the differences between races or religions, males and females think and act differently, but do so across all nationalities. Neuroscientists have identified distinct differences between the genders, and what they found is really nothing we didn't already know. It's just that now we have scientific proof.

Which gender most likely cannot find the ketchup in the refrigerator even if it is sitting on the top shelf in front of everything else? Which gender never forgets a word said in an argument and can recall details for decades? See? You already knew it was a gender thing, didn't you? No surprises, but now that we have proof there can no longer be denial. He isn't going to change and neither are you. So, best get a handle on how to go forward effectively, or forever be frustrated by the same thing over and over again.

It is important for you, as a woman, to consider these gender differences. You've been influenced by others of your gender, and also by the opposite gender. These influences greatly affect the way you think about and manage money. Whether you want to strengthen your traits or alter them, you need to identify them first. You also need to consider the differences between genders so you can interact effectively with many males in order to effectively manage your wealth.

There is nothing wrong with differences between the genders; in fact it is a good thing. Don't be mad at men for the progress they've made or the opportunities they've had. Just recognize why you may be a few steps behind – not because you are any less capable, but likely because you haven't had the same exposure to financial matters. For those of you who've already surpassed their male counterparts, you are going to be even farther ahead once you realize that you were actually handicapped this whole time. The entire female culture is looking for women like you to forge into this new territory. Your tenacity is what will change the entire financial industry for the benefit of us all.

So, why is this book just for women? First there are the physiological reasons. Humans have an innate ability to subconsciously determine threatening situations and our bodies physically respond in ways outside our conscious control. Whenever we face potential danger we get an adrenalin surge. When adrenalin surges through our bodies the only thing our mind is able to focus on is one thing – survival. You've heard of the fight or flight response. When someone scares you by surprise, do you cringe, or do you strike out? This is your body responding automatically to a potential threat. Your body does not consult with your brain during such times. In fact, all reason ceases until you are out of danger. Now, consider the environment where you often acquire financial advice or services. Often this is a one-on-one meeting with a stranger, usually a man, who does all the talking, in a small office behind a closed door. He asks personal questions for which you do not necessarily understand the reason, tries to get you to believe the way he does, and pressures you into doing things which may or may not necessarily feel comfortable. Everything your mother told you to guard against. Being alone with a strange, fast-talking man in close quarters causes an automatic physical response in women. The flighters want to run away. The fighters will stay and pay attention, but both will experience diminished ability to remain rational. This is not the best way to learn what you need to know in order to make a decision about something as important as your money.

Secondly, the financial industry was never established for women. Women have only come into financial independence in *my* lifetime. Up until I was in my mid-thirties, I could not get a loan or apply for a credit card without a male co-signer, among many other things women were prevented from doing at that time. Women today can do all these things and most women born after 1980 are unaware of what it was like for their female predecessors. So, while the financial industry has caught on to the fact that they need to change the way they market products and services to women, they haven't figured out how to effectively do that yet. Instead, women are exposed to the exact same marketing practices as men. Since males are constantly distracted, the financial industry eliminates stimuli to help them focus:

- A phone call – listening is always better for men if they can't see who they are talking to, or don't have to look at them. This is nothing new to women who have tried for years to get their husbands to look at them when they are talking, but men have an aversion to doing so for reasons I won't get into here. For a guy, investing thousands of dollars over the phone with someone they've never met is not outside their comfort zone. Is it outside yours?
- Meeting in a small room behind closed doors with another male is not outside a male's comfort zone. Is it outside yours?

The financial industry is male-dominated. Its products and services are designed to appeal to males, including educational materials, marketing messages, product literature, and service models such as cold calls, closed-door meetings, statistic sheets and financial reports – all items which do not engage the typical female mind.

The opposite sex is opposite because it is OPPOSITE.

While men need less visual stimuli, women need more. While men are attracted to numbers and statistics, women's brains go dormant at the sight. Women tend to want to explore all their options and weigh them *before* making any decisions. Women feel more comfortable in crowds and gatherings. Malls are made for women. Men prefer using one tailor, while women prefer dress shops...a lot of shops. Imagine for a moment that the only way to buy a dress is to read a manifest of all the descriptions of all the various styles from which to choose, and then make your selection based on your measurements.

As a consumer of financial products, you've been deprived of being able to shop around, compare, or even visualize what you might need, not to mention discuss it with other women who are far more likely to share similar concerns than a member of the opposite sex.

What is *your* preferred environment? Where can you best absorb information without feeling threatened? How long does it take you to ponder something before you feel ready to make a decision? Knowing these things about yourself helps you determine whether or not your financial advisors are offering you the right type of service, environment, and method that can help you rather than hinder you. Become aware of the factors which affect your decisions and start asking for them.

The financial industry is one of the most regulated industries largely because there are far too many ways to financially skin a cat . Consumers need as much protection as possible. Yet, most women rely on their financial professionals with as much trust as they have in their lover. We women have an innate need to bond with people we rely on most. Women have been known to trust even their captors and abusers out of this same tendency. When women do not have a person in their life whom they can totally trust to help them make decisions, they feel terribly abandoned which can actually cause physical stress and anxiety. This vulnerability makes women more susceptible to accepting the advice of professionals, but in doing so they place themselves in financial jeopardy. Women must guard against this tendency. Women must educate themselves and prepare adequately before soliciting any services from a financial professional. As much as I hate to admit this, all women should create a standard operating procedure to be incorporated into their wealth management plan which helps them avoid falling prey to their own natural tendencies with this regard.

Gender differences create catastrophic situations for women.

I don't have a one-way-fits-all suggestion as to how to do this, but I strongly urge you to figure out something for yourself. Some women have created a rule that whenever they feel comfortable with any financial professional, they take a long objective look at how they came to this conclusion. If their trust is based on performance and objective criteria, then fine. Trust in any financial professional should never be established on emotion or emotional comfort, but rather always on sound fact. Friends, clergy, relatives, and psychologists are all better choices for establishing trusting relationships than financial professionals who will be tempted to take advantage of your vulnerability. Later in this book you will learn more about each of the five areas of finance and the true motivations of financial professionals in each of these areas. This will help you prepare to better represent your own needs without being taken advantage of by others.

CHAPTER 4:
Where'd you get that attitude, girl?

When you were born, you had no concept of money. You had instincts for comfort, hunger, and safety. Your resources were somewhat limited: mom, dad, sister, brother, maybe a nanny. You had to rely on someone else to provide for your needs, right?

The way in which you were provided for is the way you learned about life.

- o   Fed, clothed, dry, happy....the universe is a good place.
- o   Hungry, cold, wet, crying...the universe is a bad place.

Today you are a result of all the influences and experiences you've ever had, including physical, mental, emotional and spiritual – that's a fact. But your original perception about money was not based on facts because your perceptions began before it was possible for you to comprehend the concept of money. More likely, your attitude toward money evolved as an emotion. We know it either was an extremely good emotion or an extremely bad one because our brains toss out anything mundane. We only hang onto important experiences that evoke sufficient emotion. But even a good experience can lead to poor attitudes toward money. If all you learned about money was that it made people happy, you might expect it to the same for you today, and not apply it properly to things such as providing food, shelter and safety, or postponing gratification by saving it for a large goal.

The same is true if you had a bad experience. Today you might expect that any experience concerning money is bad, and therefore want to get rid of it any way you can, or your subconscious averts any activity which might bring you more money for the fear of the potential harm that comes with it.

Neither is true. Money can be used for many good things, like providing the essentials for life; or it can be the source of very bad things, such as shopping compulsions, gambling, or delusions of false needs.

The beginning of all sound financial management is a healthy attitude about money. All too often we learn about money from negative experiences and from others who don't have a healthy attitude about money either. Psychotherapy is a process which takes people back to moments in their life which altered their behavior or response to certain stimuli in a negative way. The purpose is for them to re-examine the initial event from a different perspective and to form a new interpretation. This allows the patient to form a new opinion that can serve to generate a more appropriate response to the same stimuli. For today, focus on your attitude about money. Your money attitude was developed exactly in the same way as everything else you've come to believe and understand.

As a baby, you did not understand the United States monetary system – that's a fact!

You are not born with an understanding of money, the value of money, how it exchanges here in the United States, or how it is exchanged around the world. Yet your money attitude began the day you were born. Instantly you began to determine what is good and what is bad. By the time you experienced the exchange of something valuable for something else more valuable, you were already an expert at deciding whether you liked it, or not. From a point early in your life, your response toward money was guided by your earliest beliefs, which we know are not based on sound judgement. Since it is impossible for anyone to have based their original concepts about money on legitimate facts we all must examine our current attitudes towards money. Conscious effort is required to align yourself with the proper way to consider money – as a resource which can help you attain what you need to achieve your life goals. Without such contemplation your emotions will continue to control your behavior.

Your perception is basic to your survival. It helps you determine whether something is threatening, or not. As we mature, all our opinions compound one upon the other and form more complex perceptions, but none-the-less remain our own unique opinions, or perceptions. Facts do not matter unless we make them matter. Unless we make a conscious effort to explore the facts and form new opinions based upon facts, we remain controlled by our original perceptions, as illogical as they might be.

A healthy attitude toward money is essential to sound wealth management. Money is not the goal. It is a resource. Life is the objective. Money merely assists you in providing what you need to live a productive and fruitful life. A sound attitude promotes your ability to make good decisions about every aspect of wealth management from acquisition, to obtaining what you need, and to passing it on to others.

Does money mean power to you? Or does it mean someone else has power over you? Does money mean joy to you? Or does the lack of it mean misery? Is money elusive and unpredictable? Or is it reliable and safe? These early experiences create messages which repeat in our heads and rule our actions. Messages like:

- I have to work hard and suffer to make money.
  - Hard-working people are good people.
  - Because I endure grueling work, I am a good person.
  - If money comes too easy, something is wrong.

- Money is the root of all evil.
  - It is wrong to want money.
  - I must ignore everything about money, from making too much of it to managing it.
  - Money is bad and I should stay away from it.
- Money can buy happiness.
  - Without money I will be unhappy.
  - I must spend money to be happy.
  - I must spend money on others for them to be happy.
  - Money buys love.
- I don't need to worry about money.
  - Money management is a man's job.
    - That's a responsibility for my father, husband, son.
  - Women are to be provided for by males.
  - Money is not a woman's responsibility.
- I am not capable of taking care of my finances.
  - I've tried and I've failed.
  - All I need to do is not spend more than what I am given, which is hard.

The attitude you have toward money rules everything you do from getting a job, paying the rent, buying the shoes, going to lunch with the girls, who you marry, whether or not to divorce, and even whether you tithe a full 10-percent.

Happiness is a result of ATTITUDE, not circumstance.

Some psychologists believe that we actually seek situations to substantiate our beliefs. In other words, if we believe that money is a wonderful thing, then subconsciously we compel ourselves to seek situations in which to acquire it and enjoy it, therefore sustaining such a belief. If we believe that money is bad or will cause bad things to happen to us, or that the love of money is evil, then subconsciously we compel ourselves to seek situations in which acquiring money will cause bad things to happen to us, in which case that *also* sustains our beliefs. We will even twist things around so that nothing contradicts our beliefs. So, even if we have a good experience with money, our minds will somehow twist it around to seem bad – or vice versa.

The only way we can be certain that our attitude aligns with our conscious efforts is to identify the origin of our beliefs and examine our past actions carefully. It would be wise to incorporate an impartial third-party to help you identify your attitude toward money to avoid being tricked by your own mind. To convince you of the importance of this, I will share a personal story about a woman who believed she was doing everything right, had a very positive attitude, and never suspected she didn't possess the right attitude for her to soundly manage her money, but she paid a terrible price for that error in her judgment.

Her name was Ida. She was an 80-year old widow. It was 2007. She was nervous about her investments, just like everyone else. Her current advisor, a Certified Public Accountant with a securities license, had been a close friend of her deceased husband and managed their investments for decades. He had assured her that her investments were sound, but she didn't feel comfortable. She asked me for a second opinion. I conducted a thorough portfolio review and determined she had acquired more than enough wealth to live out the life as she desired, which included bi-annual cruises and gifting her only son $40,000 annually. Her entire portfolio was in stocks; far too risky for her relative to her needs and desires. I suggested a tax-conscious strategy to sell the stock in her portfolio, and to buy municipal and U.S. treasury bonds to minimize investment risk. She seemed comfortable with that advice, and said she would share that with her primary advisor.

She stopped back a few weeks later and told me her advisor refused to make any such changes and he had assured her once again she was fine just the way she was. He reminded her that her deceased husband used to say: "stocks are the *only* way to go." I reminded her that she had already acquired more than enough money to fulfill her needs. That she no longer needed to be exposed to such high risks. I could clearly see that she fully agreed, but she was reluctant to follow her own instincts.

I can only imagine what had influenced Ida in her past. Obviously, her husband had great influence on her, because she was still using the same financial advisor. For whatever reason, she appeared to have the opinion that she couldn't trust herself over someone else. Since she was willing to continue to follow the advice of someone who she didn't agree with instead of following her own instincts, I assume she held the belief that men are better at money matters than women.

I didn't hear from Ida again until December 2008. She called me on the phone. There was a tremble in her voice. Could I please help her, would I please meet with her? In tears, she brought me the shreds of her portfolio. There wasn't anything I could do for her by then, other than to confirm what she already knew – she lost nearly everything in the financial collapse of 2008 and was near broke. I considered her options, but the most likely was that she would have to sell her condo and move in with her son, unless she wanted to go back to work. Since she needed income from her investments to live, she was forced to pull money from what little she had left, which reduced the potential of her recovery even further, since at her age she no longer could rely on time in the market to recover her losses. Her 'financial advisors' had no suggestions, but had told her that her money would run out in less than a year.

How would this experience affect her attitude about money going forward? If she felt inept at managing her own wealth before, she is sure to feel that much more inept now. If she had discovered the origin of her attitude toward money early enough, she might have been able to alter her course. Remember, a woman's intuition is the sum of all stimuli being processed at lightning speed. It should never be ignored. Women are wired for being able to process details which are invisible to the naked eye.

Woman's intuition is the sum of all stimuli being processed at lightning speed.

Your instincts are far better than any professional advice you will ever receive from any financial professional. You already possess an innate ability to determine when you are in danger and when you are not. Proof of that is already evident – you are reading this book. You are seeking answers to things you know in your heart need to be answered. That primal instinct went off inside you and you acted upon it. This is what it feels like when your alarms go off. While you might not be able to immediately put your finger on what is wrong, your subconscious already knows something is amiss and your mind is trying to draw your attention to it to identify it and solve it.

Jokes have been made about women's instincts, but psychologists have found there is truth to them. Why? No one knows yet. Perhaps it is part of our protective instincts to protect our offspring, or some primal gene that gives us this extra power. While we don't know where we got it, we know for certain we have it. So, use it. Just make certain you function from courage and confidence, not out of fear.

Faulty attitude combined with faulty logic produces unsubstantiated fear. If fear governs your actions, you cannot trust your natural instincts. First you must re-align your beliefs and base them on facts. That takes effort and time, maybe even therapy. Do whatever you need to do to straighten out your thinking. Your life depends on it.

The difference between courage and fear is the attitude from which it evolves. Courage evolves from correct information and natural instinct. Fear evolves from incorrect information and overrides natural instinct to the point of paralysis. We all function at times from courage and at times from fear. But when fear becomes your primary driving force, it throws your entire life out of balance.

How do you know whether fear or courage is your driving force? Fear inhibits action, it is a negative power – or reaction, fear destroys a person, it does not build a person up. If you feel disempowered, it's likely fear has been driving your actions...or non-action.

Courage is a combination of having the right attitude and knowing the facts. Courage never destroys, but rather empowers action and enhances a person's capabilities. Courage is a positive power. If you feel capable of doing whatever is necessary to live your life fully, then it is likely courage has been driving your actions.

Fear debilitates.
Courage facilitates.

A mother saving her child from a speeding bus reacts out of courage, not fear. You want to react in the same way when it concerns your money...just as protectively, and out of instinct.

CHAPTER 5:
Avoid the 'shoulds' and get the goods.

Wealth management is not about budgets and sacrifices, nor is it about stocks and bonds and enhancing our wealth. Sound wealth management provides you with the peace of mind that you have everything you need to do the things most important to you throughout your life.

Sound wealth management is all about living your life fully.

The hardest part about wealth management is listening to the voice inside you...you know, that one that has been trying to be heard over the roar of your life. Stop. Listen. Get to know yourself. What is your purpose? What do you need to do here on Earth? What are your dreams? What are you all about?

The American way of life is to keep up with the Jones, but when we do, we give up our own desires and accept whatever the Jones family choses. This is a surefire way to live the wrong life and waste the only life you've been given. I want to challenge you to reconsider everything you currently believe:

- I should pay for my children's college education, because every good parent does.
- I should keep the day job and never follow my dreams, because it is foolish to give up a steady paycheck.
- My husband's and children's dreams are more important than my own.
- I should always synchronize everything I do with my spouse, because all good wives do, don't they?
- I should retire as early as possible, because everyone else wants to.
- When I retire I should buy a motor home and travel like everyone else does.
- I should leave money to my children, because they expect me to.
- I should move out of the house, because everyone tells me it is too big for one person, or the two of us.
- Alternatively, I shouldn't move out of the house when I want to because my kids can't imagine not coming home for Christmas.

Forget all those 'shoulds' and discover what is right for you, not anyone else. Form your own priorities. To become the BEST wealth manager, put your money toward YOUR life. It is that simple. To do anything else is a waste!

Live life intentionally.

The thing women should fear most is succeeding at something which doesn't really matter to them. Are you living life according to someone else's expectations, or your own?

The worst thing is to succeed at something that doesn't really matter.

First we live up to our parent's expectations, then our spouse's expectations of us, then our children's expectations, and often our friends' expectations, and certainly society's...and it starts all over again once grandchildren begin to arrive. Despite the freedoms we all have here in the United States, your self-image was not born out of freedom. Women weren't even allowed to vote for the first 143 years – tell me that didn't shape expectations.

We've been influenced from birth by others. We've been influenced positively, negatively, and ambiguously. If you haven't re-evaluated everything about your life, now is a good time to do so. The best financial advice I can give anyone is to put your money where it matters most to you. Money is a resource that can provide what you need in order to reach your desired destiny, but you *first* need to desire a destiny.

While college funding, retirement saving and health care in our old age are all worthwhile things to financially plan for, they do not represent anyone's true destiny. Typically, women want to make a difference in the lives of others; in addition to wanting a successful career or to enhance their lives with a particular pursuit, they want to be a good person, friend, daughter, wife, mother, grandmother, or neighbor. However, they are not offered help in determining what they need to do to fulfill such goals financially, but rather made to feel as though all their desires must fit into one of the four goals: college, retirement, healthcare funding, and legacy. These were made for men. Men want to keep things simple. But as we now know, women need far more options and alternative financial services to successfully reach their financial goals.

As individuals, we all have something significant which we must do to be fulfilled. What do you need to do? Think in terms of personal development: talent, achievement; or the roles you choose to fulfill in the lives of others: mother, wife, friend, artist, musician, CEO. What is your innermost desire? Is it to be free of all obligation, to feel completely confident, or is it to reign over a dynasty, rule a kingdom, serve a nation? Only your true desires should direct your wealth. Desires need not be lofty, such as seeking fame or fortune, but they need to be recognized and respected if they are ever to come true.

Too often society pressures us into living our lives in conformance to other people's values and expectations. If you succumb, you will wind up living someone else's intentions for your life instead of your own. Only you know what you truly need. No one else can tell you how to reach your destiny – only you know how to get there. Therefore, you are the only person who can direct your time, talents and resources effectively.

For more information on how to get in touch with your true desires see
ARTICLE #1: How Real Women Get what they Want at
www.RealWomenManageWealth.com

Everything you do ought to move you closer to reaching your desired destiny. Women notoriously put everyone else before themselves, and that's all right so long as it is your choice. Just make certain that you do not deny your own needs whenever you give your time, talents and resources to others.

Sacrifice is not a requirement.
It is a choice.

CHAPTER 6:
Women tell all.

As a financial advisor, I found it extremely disconcerting to realize how vulnerable women are despite financial success. Many women didn't recognize the danger they were in until it was too late. I include their stories here for your benefit. The following women all believed they were financially secure, until they weren't. Many women live with a false sense of security. I share their stories so that you will not become one of them.

Jackie was divorced with a settlement which left her a net worth of over two million. She had been a very happy CEO's wife and was shocked when he came home one day and asked for a divorce. She had no official work experience, just an old unused bachelor's degree in accounting. Their children were both in college. Her ex promised to continue to pay their children's tuition, and while that comforted her, she was annoyed at all the fun they were having at their father's new house with his new love. Broken-hearted, she consoled herself in the fact the divorce settlement at least left her financially secure for the rest of her life. That is, until unusual movements in the stock markets drew her attention in 2007 and caused her to lay awake at night worrying. She went to her financial planner. He was qualified. After all, he'd managed their marital millions for years. She trusted him. He told her not to worry. She still worried. She continued to call him, but each time he told her not to worry. She lost 50% of her investments in the crash of 2008. She went from being financially secure for the rest of her life, to not being able to maintain heat, lights and taxes on the house she had been awarded in their divorce settlement. On top of that the housing market tanked and the value of her home plummeted. She couldn't make ends meet on the interest from only half her investments. She either needed to get a job or sell the house at a loss. She took a refresher course in accounting and got a job. She is striving to get her certification as a CPA. It is her only hope of surviving in even a similar lifestyle to which she'd become accustomed. A once financially well-off executive's wife...to a working girl.

Abby was a mother of two, married for the second time to a farmer who told her if she and her children would help him work the farm, he'd take care of all her financial needs. He actually lived up to his promise. Only when he died, she discovered his definition of taking care of her financially was different than hers. His last will and testament gave her permission to live on the homestead until she died or decided to move out. That was it. No money. She had no rights to the land, so she couldn't rent it out for income. She couldn't sell the farm, take a mortgage against it, nor did she even have a say in how it was run. She was nothing but a house guest to a stepson who inherited everything. The stepson had resented her from the beginning and wasn't about to give her a dime. Neither she nor her two children, who had worked the farm for twenty years, had any entitlement to any of the assets. All she could do was live there free as long as she wished, but there was no provision for heat or lights. Only the taxes were paid by the stepson. The last I talked with her, she had found a job as a waitress at the VFW in town which was 10 miles away. Eventually she would need to move to town. Winters were too dangerous for an elderly woman to travel and remain alone in the country, but how would she afford rent? Not at all what she had intended.

Annette totally loved and trusted her husband, a sharp businessman. Even though she had been a stay-at-home mother to their four children, she had been smart enough to make certain she owned half of everything they owned. Her name was on the business, the house, both cars, and the cabin, and she made certain they had joint bank accounts. She was no dummy. When he ran off with a little tart half his age, she soon found out how well she'd managed to protect her rights. She also discovered she had no rights to prevent him from taking everything out of their joint accounts before she knew what was happening. But she got the business...boy, did she get the business. Her soon-to-be-ex ran it into the ground before they divorced just to avoid sharing the profits with her. Then he just started another business. She was left with nothing. All she has is the opportunity to claim his social security when she is old enough to retire, providing she never remarries. If she does, she will even lose that. While he enjoys his new business with a new romance, she was forced to move in with her daughter.

Speaking of an ex-husband's retirement benefit, **Judy**, who was divorced for more than 30 years tried to collect on her ex-husband's social security benefits when she turned 66, which the law allows, only to discover that she signed the divorce decree six months too soon. To be eligible to receive an ex-spouse's social security benefits you need to have been married for a minimum of 10 years.

Even when he would walk on hot coals for you, things can still go awry.

Deb was happily married to a wonderful man. They had two children. They lived in a modest home in a pleasant part of town and both worked. Life was good. Then Deb's mother passed away and she inherited $100,000. She wanted a new home, a bigger house, one with an attached garage and a bigger kitchen. She figured that if they sold the one they were in and used just a little from her inheritance, they could get a bigger house while still putting most of her inheritance toward their retirement fund. They both agreed on the plan, and he would handle all the financial aspects. When they couldn't find an existing home that suited them, they decided to build. Her head soon began to burst with ideas on how to make it their perfect living space. Each idea had a cost, but her husband didn't object. He agreed to every idea she came up with and never once brought up the added cost. After all it was her inheritance; she was the one who wanted the house. All he wanted to do was to make her happy...and, boy, was she happy…until all the money was gone. When she discovered that not only was the inheritance gone, but all their savings and he'd taken an additional line of credit on the house, she was livid. Their relationship was strained to the breaking point. She couldn't forgive him for not telling her that the construction on the new house was eating up all their money. He had no idea that having that money in the bank had given her a sense of security. He thought all she wanted was the home of her dreams, and he was doing everything to give it to her. While she couldn't forgive him for spending all their money, he couldn't understand why she wasn't happy – gender differences.

I could go on and on, but while I can't forget the hundreds of stories women have told me, you don't need to listen to them all to understand the point I'm trying to make. You need to take money management seriously, whether or not you have someone else currently in your life doing so.

CHAPTER 7:
Have it your way.

Money is a resource. No one needs a piece of paper or an inedible metal object, but having money allows us to access the things we desire. Money is used as an exchange for goods and services. It is easier to purchase food, shelter, and safety instead of trading chickens or goats. Money allows us access to experiences that add meaning to our lives, such as time with loved ones, education, and can provide the tools we need from a professional wardrobe to gardening shears.

When our lives become the primary objective of our pursuits, our time, talents and resources funnel correctly. This is why it is important for you to know what your true objectives are for your life. Without that information, one of your most valuable resources – money – flounders in providing what you need to fulfill yourself.

To effectively manage money, you need to know for what you need it, when you need it, and how much you will need. Therefore, the first thing you need to know about sound wealth management is why you need money. Not why everyone else needs money, but why *you* need it.

By knowing what your needs are and what you want to accomplish in life, you will make better decisions with regard to your money throughout your journey. Money ebbs to and flows from us all throughout life. What we do to initiate and maintain these ebbs and flows is what wealth management is all about. Sometimes we have too much flow and not enough ebb, or too much ebb and not enough flow. And because there are stages our lives go through, how we manage money also goes through stages. Early in life we accumulate more money than we spend, or at least we should. Later in life we spend more money than we accumulate. After we're gone, we leave whatever is left behind. You have made decisions about your money all throughout these stages whether you've realized it or not. No plan is still a plan. Not a good plan, but none-the-less it is a choice. Being cognizant of our decisions is the first lesson in wealth management. What are you doing with your money? Does this match what you should be doing with your money in order to achieve your primary objectives?

Women notoriously avoid setting personal goals largely because our current society places a value on women's roles as nurturers and supportive companions versus individual achievers. For those whose only goal is to cater to the whims of others, you still need to determine what those whims might be and when they might occur. For those who juggle their own personal goals with that of everyone else's in their lives, clearly identifying your own objectives will help you determine better guidelines for all the things you want to accomplish. For those of you who fall into the category of individual achievers, identifying your specific goals will advance your efforts immensely.

Setting and attaining goals is a learned skill. Males are more exposed to such skill-building opportunities all throughout life in a variety of ways from interests in sports to on-the-job experiences. Females, however, not only lack exposure to such tactics, but also lack role models, encouragement and support from their peers. As a result, women are less apt to set proper goals.

Compounding the barriers for women is the fact that the current financial service models focus only on a few objectives: college funding for children, retirement, long term care, and legacy. While many of these same objectives are likely to be part of your financial plan, they do not cover the issues which concern most women, such as: feeling financially secure, wanting to make a difference in the lives of others, and living life to its fullest. These types of goals require different approaches which require different products and services which haven't yet been developed.

So, where does a woman start? At the beginning, of course. Sound wealth management is a process which begins by identifying the ultimate destination, then plans an appropriate route to reach it. How does one set a financial goal? You set a personal goal and find out the cost of achieving that goal. Example:

- My goal is to be the best mother I can be.
  o Food, shelter and safety for a minimum of 18 years for each child.
  o Buy a home in a good school district with a backyard.
  o Provide annual family vacations and other unifying experiences.
  o Provide post-secondary education for all my children.
  o Provide special occasions, such as graduations and weddings.
- My goal is to feel financially self-sufficient.
  o Determine my current financial situation.
  o Understand what my financial needs are for the rest of my life.
  o Identify probable sources of income throughout my life.
  o Create a plan of action which best utilizes my current financial situation and all potential resources throughout my life, and review this plan at least annually to adjust it, or refine it.
- My goal is to become an Olympic gymnast.
  o Hire a good coach.
  o Acquire a suitable place to practice.
  o Sacrifice time, effort and resources to develop a talent.
  o Attend competitions around the world.
  o Pay the entrance fees to athletic events.

By identifying your goals you can better determine what needs to be done and calculate potential costs. Once you know what each of your intentions will cost, you can determine where you will obtain the funds to support each goal. By reviewing your goals regularly, you can best manage all your resources: time, talents, and money.

Goal-setting is imperative to sound wealth management. In fact, unless you have specific goals, there is no point in reading the rest of this book. Without a target, there is nothing to shoot for. Without specific goals you are at the mercy of others, and they are at the mercy of you – since you require money to survive whether you do so efficiently, or not. Everyone alive is either a financial help or a hinderance to themselves and others.

Having specific goals enables you to determine appropriate courses of action to achieve them. According to scientific research, writing them down doubles your success rate. By merely writing down your goals you process them from the creative side of your brain to the logical side your brain. This action alone translates your goal to a command and activates both the conscious and subconscious aspects of your brain. Unless you change that command, your brain will not rest until it is fulfilled. Therefore, achieving goals is as simple as writing them down on a piece of paper. This comes in handy when it comes to communicating your goals to others. For now, let's just concentrate on identifying your goals and writing them down.

Women have been discouraged from identifying their goals by the entire financial industry which focuses on college, home purchases, retirement, healthcare funding, and legacy. But while women share these aspirations, women have far more specific goals which need to be addressed, such as:

- I want to feel financially secure.
- I want to be financially independent of others.
- I want to be remembered as a good person (mother, grandmother, aunt, daughter, sister, friend, wife.)
- I want to feel confident that I won't run out of money before I die.
- I want to provide my child with incentive to fulfill their own aspirations.

These are all reasonable and achievable financial goals. Even though the entire financial industry is unable to help you, I will show you how you can help yourself. But first, you need to have goals – written ones.

> For additional help in learning to set personalized goals
> see *ARTICLE #1: How Real Women Get What They Want*
> at www.RealWomenManageWealth.com

As a financial advisor, I met with couples to plan for retirement. Countless times I witnessed the wife nearly fall off her chair when I asked them to explain exactly what they intended to do in retirement. More often the guy had completely different ideas than his wife ever imagined.

- One couple: his idea was to sell the house and move to the cabin to fish and hunt all day; whereas his wife had no intention of selling the house in which she'd raised her children and was looking forward to spending time with grandchildren in that very same house.
- Another couple: his idea was to sell the house and buy a motor home and travel the nation; whereas the wife had no interest in any sort of travel that didn't include room service.

Retirement is no different than anything in life. It means something different to everyone. What I noticed between the genders, however, is men tend to have very vague ideas, but which alter lifestyles more dramatically, and they often want to sell the house. Women tend to have more personalized and specific intentions which are less likely to disrupt the lifestyle to which she has become accustomed. Her expectations are to spend more time with loved ones and doing volunteer work. The thing I noticed about both genders is neither communicated their intentions to their spouses any better than the other.

Planning for retirement is vastly different between the genders. For example, men do not imagine décor when they imagine their preferred living arrangements, while women do. In fact, men don't necessarily even imagine a roof over their heads. Tents, fishing shacks, hunting blinds, and motorhomes more often are part of their desired environments, whereas women tend to want safe, warm, inviting environments in which to host family and friends for memorable experiences. Often women desire a complete re-do of their environment which includes new carpet, drapes and upgrades in appliances, much to the utter shock of their husbands who believe they will never need to buy another sofa once they retire.

It isn't that women are any less eager to plan for the future, it is that the current methods for doing so bore them to death.

Most couples are not aware they are out of sync with one another. Differences between the genders affects their ability as a couple to achieve any mutual financial goals. When a woman isn't clear about what she wants, she will not only inadvertently sabotage her own intentions, but her husband's as well. Remember, women make 80% of all household purchase decisions. What a waste of valuable resources for both.

The mission of every business is to provide a specific product or service to a specific market. When the business plan includes a vision of where the business should go in the future, it is far more likely that decisions all along the way will promote that vision. Good business plans include written goals which need to be reached to achieve that ultimate vision. These written goals are what guides the entire company from start-up to conglomerate. These written goals are used to determine whether or not the current operations are achieving progress, or not. Written goals promote clear communication. While they can be changed and altered, goals must always be written. And that's the point I want to make here.

Most people don't run their lives like a business, but successful ones do. Successful people know that goals are integral to guiding their lives exactly the same way business goals guide a company. Men are naturally more exposed to goal-setting than women due to everything from sports to corporate experiences. While they may not be any better at writing out their goals than women, these experiences still have a positive influence on the way they think.

No one is eager to make sacrifices for no reason. Since males are not as detail oriented, vague financial goals are suitable. But for women, who require a lot of stimuli before they engage, vague financial goals feel boring and seem unattainable. When women are not actively engaged in saving for future goals, they run the risk of developing habits which undermine themselves and their households. However, once women are given the opportunity to visualize their true desires, they demonstrate far better wealth management skills than their counterparts.

Instead of planning to bulk save for a child's college funding, women tend to think of it as a series of things, such as:

- I want to provide my child with emotional support during their college years. Your plan might need to include communication and travel costs for both you and your child, depending on who needs to see or talk to whom the most and how often.
- I want to provide my child with suitable attire when they begin college. If you can't stand the thought of your child being anything but chic, you have a whole new item to cover in planning for your child's education.
- I want to give my child occasional respite from academic studies and pay for spring break vacations. That calculates differently whether that means Cancun or Ohio.
- I want to see my child walk across a stage to receive their diploma. Better include travel funds for yourself in that college funding plan for your child.

Do you see how by visualizing in this manner offers more incentive to work with financial professionals? The bland method men use just isn't very exciting to most women who require far more stimuli.

While the current financial planning opportunities are sufficient for most males who just want to know a vague financial target to shoot for, women require something entirely different. So far, the financial industry doesn't offer any such support for women. Largely because women, themselves, don't yet know what they need. However, as more and more women become aware of what they truly need and want, their demands will alter the current financial services industry. One can only imagine what it will look like in decades to come, but one thing is certain – it won't be the same.

Whatever you do, do not allow the current method of setting financial goals inhibit you. I suggest a brainstorming session just to get started. Take a sheet of paper and number it to 100. Set the timer on your stove for 30 minutes and try to fill all the blanks with things you would like to accomplish before you die. Don't think too hard or long about anything, just try to fill all 100 answers before time is up. Then, take a look at what you wrote, circle the ones most interesting to you, embellish them and turn them into your goals. These are the reasons you need money.

Money is not the objective.

Money is not the goal. Living your life is the goal. Money is a resource which provides a means to obtain what you need to live your life fully. All your resources, your time, talents and money, ought to go toward achieving your goals. To manage your money wisely to that end you first need to know your goal. Have I said this enough times? It is important that you write down your goals.

For additional help in learning to set personalized goals
see *ARTICLE #1: How Real Women Get What They Want*
at www.RealWomenManageWealth.com

CHAPTER 8:
Bank on it.

Banks are used primarily for cash flow, loans, and credit cards. Most people understand that, but few realize that banks also offer tax shelters, investments, and can even substitute the need for costly legal documents such as power of attorney, trusts and wills.

One of the most misused and misunderstood benefits a bank offers is 'account titling'. All bank accounts are governed by law according to the way they are titled. An 'account title' is the way in which you open the account: single, joint, etc. By titling an account correctly, you can protect the funds in that account, or if you don't do it correctly, you can bind yourself into a legal hell.

Bank accounts are governed by regulation and law: tax laws, estate laws and laws which govern the way in which such accounts can be used.

Law prevails according to the way in which an account is titled.

The way in which you open an account determines how that account will function under the law. Whether it be a deposit account, such as a checking or savings account, an investment account opened as a traditional Individual Retirement Account (IRA), or Roth Account, a credit card, or a loan, such as a mortgage or auto loan...the way in which you title the account when you open it determines how the law treats it from then on. You can't just go back and make changes whenever you want. So, make certain when you open any account, including loans, that you title them for your own benefit. Remember, this course is not about making everyone else in your life comfortable – it is about protecting YOU.

Allow me to explain a few ways in which you can title an account, and hopefully this will open your eyes to the many ways in which account titling can assist you.

- **Individual or single bank account**: is set up in one person's name only and can only be accessed by that one person. Single people generally use this form of titling. Also, people wishing to prevent anyone else from accessing such funds, such as their spouse or significant other, also use this type of titling. Upon death, the funds are held in estate until legal matters are settled.

While it might be tempting for a college student to use this type of account given their independence, it still may be beneficial to share a joint account with a parent they trust to take care of financial matters in lieu of more costly legal documents, such as a will or a power of attorney.

- **Joint Account:** is set up so that two or more people have full access to the funds. The funds belong entirely to all parties listed as joint owners and can be accessed by any party at any time without restriction.

Most married couples open joint accounts. However, if there is no will in place upon the death of one of the owners the account funds are held in estate, or 'frozen', until the executor of the estate determines what portion belongs to the estate and what portion belongs to the other co-owners. A spouse could find themselves in a real pickle trying to pay monthly bills without access to that checking or savings account. Generally with couples, the surviving joint owner is often the executor for the deceased owner and can provide the bank with adequate information to free the funds in a relatively short period of time, but if that isn't the case between you and your spouse, or neither of you yet have a will, this account would go through probate which could tie it up for years. Also, should one of you acquire dementia, this type of titling on your accounts could be a detriment. As a joint-owner, you are vulnerable to anything your co-owner has a mind to do – such as write a check for big boat, or run off with all your money before you know it. Titling of your accounts needs to be reviewed and managed accordingly. See your banker to learn more about the different ways in which you can title an account, and the laws surrounding them.

It may be wise to visit your attorney prior to opening your bank accounts. Certainly, the titling of your bank accounts should be conveyed to your attorney at some point to make certain you are legally protected the way in which you desire.

Also, you should be aware of the fees, penalties and other costs associated with bank products and services. Retail banks are not a public service. They are in business to make money. Their products are checking, savings and credit card accounts, in addition to lending accounts.

In addition to providing customers with cash flow options, banks also offer investment and tax products. Banks sell certificates of deposit for that particular bank. Some banks also offer government zero coupon bonds. For small amounts it is all right to buy these investments directly from your bank; however, in most cases it is better to purchase these products through your investment advisor as she can lower the risk even further by diversifying them among more than one bank and by spreading them over a wider region.

Your banker also offers tax shelters, but always meet with a qualified tax advisor before opening a tax shelter.

There are two types of banks: 'Commercial retail' banks, which are depository banks and lending banks; and 'investment' banks. While they each can be under the same roof, they should be regarded by consumers as two entirely different firms – which they technically are.

Commercial retail banks are generally what we think of when we think 'bank.' It is what we are talking about here. Investment banks are usually thought of as 'investment firms.'

Each type of bank offers financial products which function similarly, but are radically different. Be aware of which type of bank you are doing business with before you do business. We will talk more about investment banks in Chapter 10.

The primary take-away about retail banking is:

1. Account titling can be used to manage many complex legal situations. An attorney isn't your only solution. Sometimes your banker can do the same thing for far less cost, but always seek the advice of a qualified lawyer before you choose to title your account for any particular purpose. Go back and forth between your banker and your lawyer until you are comfortable making a decision.

2. Bank products include tax shelters and investments, but one should always obtain the advice of a qualified tax expert and/or an investment professional before choosing to buy these types of products from a retail bank. Once you have the advice of a tax advisor, visit your banker to open the appropriate type of account.

3. There are two types of banks – retail and investment – and never should you confuse the two. A retail bank offers deposit accounts and loans. An investment bank deals in securities, stock and bonds, and other products with more risk. Each is regulated differently.

4. Loans, interest rates, penalties, fees, and other costs to banking should all be considered when choosing services or products from a bank.

See *ARTICLE #6: How Real Women Utilize Banking Strategies* at www.RealWomenManageWealth.com

CHAPTER 9:
Guard yourself right.

The funny thing about insurance is that people are *more* likely to properly insure the least important things, and *least* likely to insure the *most* important things. When it comes to buying auto insurance, they fully cover a brand new $50,000 automobile with comprehensive coverage, and they take only liability insurance on the junkers. But rarely do they assess their own value adequately.

The average wage-earner making $50,000 a year income will bring in over $2,000,000 in their lifetime. The potential earning of a wage-earner should determine the amount of insurance they need.

Your health and ability to create income, manage wealth, and provide sustainable services for yourself and others *are* your most valuable assets. If you are not employed outside the home, you are a money-saving machine and the value of the services you bring should be the determining factor. Either way, health, disability and life insurance are essential until you no longer bring any monetary value to your household, and then you need healthcare insurance to avoid losing everything you've worked to obtain, and/or to avoid becoming a financial detriment to yourself and others.

In all my experience as a financial advisor, I never once conducted an insurance evaluation that was correct. Either people have too much insurance, or not enough...or not enough of the right type of insurance.

The reason most people don't have the right amount of life insurance is they are sold insurance by insurance agents. Insurance is sold by creating fear of loss. It is also sold by creating greed. However, the only thing that should determine what type and the amount of insurance you need is a legitimate financial need.

See your local insurance agent for collateral insurance (home, auto, boat and motorcycle), your human services department for health and disability insurance (group plans offer potential benefits), but your investment advisor is the best person to go for life and long- term care insurance as well as other hybrids which may provide additional benefits to your particular financial situation, and annuities. Though these are insurance products, your investment advisor is less likely to sell you more insurance than you need and is better able to help you use insurance as a financial planning tool.

As your obligations to others ceases and/or your assets increase in value, so should your need for insurance. Re-evaluate the need for insurance at least every five years.

Your need for insurance changes throughout your life.

Because the death benefit of an insurance policy currently passes to heirs tax free, insurance policies are used as financial planning tools to provide heirs with enough funds to pay anticipated estate taxes, thereby replacing the value of one's estate.

So what should you do? First consult your tax advisor to learn more about the estate tax laws in your state and the current federal laws which might affect you and your heirs. Then, consider whether an additional insurance policy is a good solution. Again, your investment advisor may be a good resource for helping you make such decisions.

Other things you should know about insurance policies:

- Death benefits pass to heirs tax free.
- Death benefits paid to beneficiaries of insurance policies are not probated, nor required to be made public.
  - o If you want one heir to get more money than another heir, you can use your wealth to buy life insurance policies which pay different death benefits and designate the beneficiaries however you wish as a means of transferring your wealth privately.
- Annuities are insurance policies which can create lifetime streams of income. If the company you work for doesn't pay a pension, you can create one for yourself by buying an annuity.

While we're on the subject of annuities there are a few things you ought to understand. An annuity is a contract which you buy– you don't invest into an annuity – you buy it. It's a contract. Once you pay for it, the insurance company has your money and you have their agreement that says they will pay you back in a certain amount in certain installments for a certain period of time at a certain interest rate, providing they are able to do so. The risk of an annuity is the financial stability of the issuing insurance company. An annuity is basically a paid-up insurance policy that has an elaborate contract benefit, a potential tax benefit, and a death benefit.

The risk associated with an annuity is the financial stability of the issuing insurance company.

There is a lot more you need to know about annuities before you buy them, but it is not the purpose of this book to tell you everything about them here. Rather, the purpose of this book is to make you aware of some things enough to encourage you to explore matters further on your own and to help you identify where to find such information. See your investment advisor for more information about annuities, and shop around before you buy.

Insurance products protect assets in the event of a catastrophe – which happens to everyone throughout life for reasons we'd rather ignore. But sound wealth management does not ignore potential danger. It plans for it. How have you planned for life?

Insurance products are far more diverse than what most people realize. However, if you go to an insurance agent, you likely will be sold on something you may not need. A better place to shop for insurance is through an investment advisor who is licensed to sell stocks, not just mutual funds (be sure to ask). An investment advisor who is properly licensed to sell securities has access to more diverse insurance products which may be right for you, while an insurance agent is limited in what they can offer.

See *ARTICLE #7: How Real Women Buy Insurance,* and
ARTICLE #8: How Real Women Shop for Investment Advice
at www.RealWomenManageWealth.com

CHAPTER 10:

Be a pest before you invest.

Most people do not initially realize how much knowledge is required to properly coordinate the five pillars of finance: banking, insurance, investments, taxes and law. Yet when you mention wealth management, most people think of only one aspect: investments. Investments are the least important to acquiring wealth and managing it effectively. If you don't coordinate all the other pillars pertinent to your situation you are at risk of not making as much as you could, and you have an increased risk of losing it all.

Investing is taking what you can afford to lose and placing it at risk in order to wind up with more money than if you didn't.

Investing should come after everything else: after banking, insurance, taxes and law. It makes no sense to invest your money with the hopes of making 10 percent on your investments while losing 50 percent to taxes; or risking everything because of improper banking practices, lack of proper protection, or not having the law on your side.

For the sake of getting to the point of this chapter, let's assume your financial affairs are in order and you know exactly what you can afford to risk, how long you can risk it, and can clearly define why you want to risk it.

Before you consider any type of investment it is wise to know a little something about the world of investments. While the concept of exchanging one thing for another has been around since cave-dwellers traded rocks for feathers, civilized man did not trade stocks until the 1600s, prompted by the spice trade in the Netherlands. Eventually England became the seat for such stock trade, which is how the concept came to America. While the practice was limited to wealthy tycoons up to that point, our colonial government financed the Colonial War by selling bonds – mere pieces of paper which declared that a group of guys who *we* regarded as our leaders at the time, promised to pay out at a profit at a later date – assuming we won the war. Had we not won the war, those bonds would have defaulted and our unofficial government, which would have gone defunct, would have paid out nothing.

The same thing happened during our Civil War. There are people who still hold worthless Confederate Bonds hoping the South will rise again. As an investor, you give power to anything you invest into. Had it not been for investors, we might never have become a nation.

When our colonial government began selling bonds to raise money for the war, it also put a few bees in the bonnets of bankers who saw an opportunity for themselves. They came up with a scheme which made them richer by issuing stocks, or shares to raise their own money. By 1792 this practice was in full swing in New York – our nation's capital at the time. A group of men met daily on the corner of Wall and Broad Streets in New York City to trade stocks and bonds – under umbrellas or wrapped in wool scarves. They created a new market which became known as the New York Stock Exchange.

You promote the underlying entity of whatever you invest into.

When the United States began experiencing rapid immigration and growth in the mid-1800s, companies needed funds to expand their business in order to meet the increasing demands of consumers. These same companies also realized that investors would be interested in owning a piece of their pie, so they began selling shares of their companies. By 1921 millions of dollars were being traded daily on the corner of Wall and Broad Streets, and it was time to move in out of the rain and cold. 40 Wall Street became the site of the New York Stock Exchange, where it remains today.

The industrial revolution brought new interest in trading as people began to realize that profits could be made by re-selling the stock to others who saw value in a company. This opened what is called a Secondary Market known also as the 'speculators market.' It was more volatile because it was fueled by 'highly subjective speculation' versus more objective aspects about a company's financial stability and future potential. But that's when the music began to play – The Roaring Twenties! What had been a hobby for the rich suddenly was available to the average person, and soon everyone was making money the easy way – by investing. *Smart* people owned stock versus traditional assets like land or a house. Our nation became rich beyond anyone's imagination. Nobody worked any more. They partied. Everyone had nannies, cooks and housekeepers--even the nannies, cooks and housekeepers. Women had time for glamour and wore long gowns and smoked cigarettes from long cigarette holders. Men wore tuxedos and spats, smoked cigars in drawing rooms while they talked investments, and everyone was happy until the party suddenly stopped on Tuesday, October 29, 1929.

The banks, which started this whole idea of trading stocks in the first place, had speculated with their depositor's money and lost. Not only did investors lose everything, but all the little old widows and conservative men who had deposited their life savings in the bank because they were too afraid to take the risks of investing it – they lost everything, too. The banks could no longer cover those deposits. The banks had blown everyone's money in the stock market, not just the investments investors had made, but everyone's savings.

Some people think if they put money into a checking or savings account that it is held in a vault at that bank. It's not. It leaves that bank in less than twelve hours and is used on the world exchange for a bunch of different reasons, none of which is to hold it safely for you until you need it. Depositors back in 1929 learned that lesson the hard way.

Your money isn't being kept in a vault at the bank.

A run on the banks occurred as people clamored to get what they could out of the bank before it ran dry. After that, people were afraid to put their money into bank accounts. Instead, they stuffed it into mattresses. But when money sits in mattresses it can't be lent out in mortgages, business loans, or cash flow to companies who need to make payroll. This fear fouled up the entire economy.

Our nation plunged into what would become known as the Great Depression as a result of this one event. However, since 75% of the people still had income, and because people still had a little egg money – stashes they had kept for a rainy day, and because people couldn't comprehend what actually happened nor how it would affect their lives, they went right on living the same old way until they lost their jobs, used up all their cash, and were forced to sell their homes and everything they owned. It took years before the majority of the population – particularly non-investors – to realize what actually happened in 1929. Meanwhile, while they plunged into poverty. Those who realized early on what was happening capitalized on the situation and survived a whole lot better than those who did not. Wealth management requires being aware of what is happening around you and understanding how it impacts you and your household, and being able to adjust quickly.

By 1935, 25% of our nation fell into total poverty, and the other 75% took in family members to feed and clothe which they hadn't planned on. There was no Social Security, Medicare, or Health and Human Services, or even food shelves. The Salvation Army and Missions who had served the derelicts of society suddenly swelled with demand from former middle-class Americans who no longer had a penny to their name. Men who had once been well-respected – husbands, fathers, former home-owners – hopped trains in search of jobs and were forced to leave their families behind. These once well-respected men of society became known as hobos. Most never returned to their families because there were no jobs to be found anywhere...for years. Eventually women were forced to give their children away or leave them with relatives or neighbors while they, too, searched for work in bigger cities once they realized their husbands were not coming back. Children were left in orphanages, some were put on orphan trains with the hopes that someone somewhere across this vast nation would take them in and feed them. Times became desperate for many people.

How long could you survive without any income? Without any money? How bad would it have to get before you would consider giving your children away just so they could eat? This happened to people just like you because they were unable to comprehend what was going on in the world around them until it was too late.

One out of every four households lost their income by 1932, and the other three out of four lost all trust in banks. Government was desperate to spur people's confidence and get them to start depositing money back into the banks once again. They commissioned FDIC, the Federal Deposit Insurance Corporation, which guarantees your money is safe once you deposit it into a retail bank which is FDIC insured. That got people going to banks once again, which invigorated lending and stimulated the economy.

To promote further trust, the government formed the Securities and Exchange Commission (SEC) and Congress passed the Banking Act of 1933, which contained regulation which divided banks according to their primary practices; either they were a savings and lending institution, or they were an investment institution. That single piece of legislation prevented these banks from ever crossing the line again, amen. While that prevented us from disaster for 75 years, it was repealed in 2000 and once again retail banks climbed into bed with investment banks.

In less than eight years we blew ourselves up once again, only this time worse than before because now we are a global economy. What happens to us in the United States affects every single living soul on earth, from New York to the jungles of the Amazon. We are still suffering the aftermath of the Global Financial Collapse of 2008. Just like the folks in 1929 who didn't realize what was happening until it was too late, millions of people are exposed to a similar fate today either directly due to loss of job, wages, or worse; or indirectly as they take on added financial responsibility for other family members due to a weak economy. The saving grace of society today is this time we have some social programs already in place, which prevented a similar situation which caused lengthy soup lines and orphan trains during the 30s. Unemployment, bankruptcy options, Social Security, Medicaid, Health and Human Services, and local food shelves absorb those who suffer today. This deprives the rest of the population the visual effect that soup lines and orphan trains once had. The economy is just as bad, only it doesn't impact our society in the same way it once did.

Had it not been for Barack Obama, who was running as a candidate for the President of the United States in 2008 and who was the only one with the foresight to have a plan in place in case of just such a catastrophe (unlike anyone else in politics at the time, including then-President George W. Bush), every single American citizen would be out a minimum of $500,000 - half a million dollars each. If that was your entire net worth in 2008, you'd be homeless today. What he did was ingenious and I wish I could explain all the details, but again, that's not the purpose of this book. You will have to research it on your own, and I encourage you to do so because not only is it captivating, it will show you the value of regulation. Putting politics aside, we all should be grateful for how that was handled.

The same was true in 1929 as in 2008 as it is today. Most people don't understand how they participate in world economics, nor how global economics affects their lives. When citizens are ignorant about such important facts, they become part of the problem instead of part of the solution. This same mentality plagues our nation today. It is difficult to decipher between fact and fiction when you are unfamiliar with the elements which have the most effect on your financial situation, such as taxation and politics relative to domestic and world economics. Simply put: when the majority is healthy, wealthy and wise, everyone in the nation benefits. When the majority is unhealthy, poor and ignorant, everyone in the nation suffers. It isn't quantum physics.

Wall Street is complicated, but it is just one of hundreds of stock exchanges around the world, all humming and drumming at the same time: The American Stock Exchange, the Chicago Board of Exchange, the London Stock Exchange, Japan, Hong Kong...the list is long. It is impossible for any *one* person to comprehend the magnitude of what is happening through these exchanges every second of every business day. Investing isn't like going to the casino and testing your luck. It is a highly complicated system which interacts with other highly complicated systems which are designed to work well for everyone, but which rarely do. Luck has no place in investing.

You've seen the frenzy on the trading floor on the news from time to time; well that's an everyday occurrence at the hundreds of stock exchanges throughout this country and around the world. You can't imagine the activity generated in an up-tic or a down-tic, so don't even try. This industry moves at such a rapid pace that no other profession can compare, with the possible exception of a trauma unit at an emergency hospital during a major tragic event.

The financial world is bigger than any single person can comprehend well enough to give anyone else solid answers to anything, but people will try to convince you otherwise. The best you can do is obtain the best advice you can get when you need it and hope it is sufficient. Clearly conveying your objectives is the key to obtaining good advice, see Chapter 7.

Professional investment advisors are an essential resource, but finding the right one is near impossible unless you know how to qualify them relative to your specific needs, and you are willing and able to consistently monitor their behavior.

Research several types of investment firms. Investment firms vary in the scope of the types of investments and services they are allowed by law to provide, the types of research they conduct, the way they are compensated, who regulates them, and much more. There is a plethora of information on this on the internet and at your local library, but you need not be an expert on anything other than knowing your own personal goals and objectives at any given time.

A few things to know about the various types of investment banks: some have their own analysts and economists which provide clients with exclusive reports; most firms have a specific list of companies which they evaluate thoroughly as part of the process of promoting stock in those same companies; some firms have an actual seat on an exchange and can offer initial public offerings while other firms do not. This is how the big money is made on Wall Street.

Most investment banks require a minimum to open an investment account of between $500,000 to $1 million in investable assets, but you better have considerably more if you want their best attention. Smaller firms are willing to open accounts for less, but they cannot offer the same quantity, and perhaps quality, of analysis reports nor as many types of investment options. Let your own sophistication level guide you. If you don't know what a derivative is, then you don't need a firm on Wall Street. A Main Street investment shop that specializes in mutual funds is a good fit for most people, but not for everyone. If you still don't know which firm is right for you, ask questions of all types of firms until you understand.

Once you select an appropriate investment bank for your needs, begin interviewing advisors within that firm. A potential advisor will be interviewing you for a good fit for the same reason you will be interviewing her. Not all advisors seek additional clients, and no advisor is obligated to take on any client they believe is not a right fit for them. There should be compatibility between the client and the advisor based on experience, need, and ability to communicate effectively.

To help you navigate among all the titles and credentials you will come across, there are a few things you need to understand about all investment advisors:

- Some titles are acquired by passing an exam and obtaining a license:
  - Registered Representative
  - Registered Investment Advisor
- Some titles are given by a broker-dealer:
  - Stock broker
  - Sales Associate
- Some titles have absolutely no legal meaning or imply any credibility whatsoever:
  - Financial Advisor
  - Financial Specialist
- Some titles are given when certain sales quotas are reached:
  - Vice-President of Investments
  - Senior Financial Advisor
  - Senior Financial Specialist

The point is, all financial titles are a bit dubious because all financial professionals are sales people first and foremost, but they all like to imply something other than the fact they are out to sell you as much as you are willing to buy.

In addition to the many titles one can purport, there is a litany of credentials and designations available to advisors. While some are obtained by fulfilling educational requirements and passing exams, these credentials do not necessarily mean the bearer performs any of the duties one might expect. See more about this in Chapter 13.

You should also be familiar with the various aspects of the investment industry in order to determine a good fit for yourself. Prepare yourself enough about the following subjects to understand your own needs relative to the type of products and service each candidate can provide. Then ask a lot of questions on your quest.

1. **Investment philosophies, methods and theories:** Which do you prefer your investment advisor to follow?
2. **Rules, regulations, laws, licensing, education and other standards to which an investment advisor may be held responsible:** Depending on the type of products and/or services you require, what qualifications should you be looking for in an investment advisor?
3. **Certifications, designations and other credentials:** What, if any, additional credentials might your situation require?
4. **Compensation method:** Would you be best served by a commission-based or fee-based advisor, or a combination?
5. **Code of Ethics:** To what professional standards of conduct or code of ethics do they adhere? How would you seek remedy in the event of a complaint?
6. **Background check:** Have any complaints been filed or sanctions put on this advisor? If so, for what, when, and how did it come out?
7. **Experience**: Don't even bother asking about their tenure. Experience counts for little in the investment industry because investment advisors are merely salespeople. The more experience they have only means they are good at selling securities. They are all trained adequately to sell.

See *ARTICLE #8: How Real Women Shop For Investment Advice* at www.RealWomenManageWealth.com

Once you select an investment advisor, it is essential you are completely candid with her about everything, including all your investments, your health and longevity expectations, and any concerns. Financial professionals abide by ethics standards of confidentiality. The more they know about you, the better they can help you.

Once you choose an investment advisor that advisor should be able to educate you about anything and everything pertinent to any decision you have to make. If you do not feel confident in making a decision – your answer should be 'no, thank you.' You always have the right to seek a second opinion from another advisor from another firm, or within that same firm.

Remember, your wealth is your responsibility, no one else's. You will either reap the rewards or bear the consequences of how you manage your wealth.

Investing is making money by using the money you already have to do so.

I always imagine every dollar that comes my way as a little green minion who I can put to work to make me more money. If I don't put my minion to work, they lose money by not keeping up with inflation. If I work my minions too hard, I could work them to death and they will leave me altogether. Finding the right work-pace for my minions is the key.

You are the boss of your little green minions. Putting your little green minions to work requires that each team of minions have specific instructions for how hard and how long to work in order to complete their purpose. While you remain the boss, you hire a supervisor for your minions – an investment advisor. Your investment advisor develops a work schedule for each team of minions and oversees their progress, but you remain the person in charge of them all – you are the BOSS. Therefore, it is necessary to periodically check on everyone's performance and make necessary adjustments to maximize everyone's efforts to fulfill your goals.

See *ARTICLE #8: How Real Women Shop for Investment Advice* at
www.RealWomenManageWealth.com

Financial Security
Once and **For All** and **Forever**
How *Real* Women Manage Wealth

The following articles support the topics found in this book in more detail and are available for purchase at:

www.RealWomenManageWealth.com

Article # 1 How Real Women Get What They Want
Identify what you really want out of life.

Article # 2 How Real Women Adapt Gender Differences
Recognize the power and limitations of being a woman.

Article # 3 How Real Women Guard Against Sales Tactics
Protect yourself from people capitalizing on your vulnerabilities.

Article # 4 How Real Women Vote
Understand the impact government has on your personal wealth.

Article # 5 How Real Women Treat Tax Laws
Maximize tax advantages for every stage of life.

Article # 6 How Real Women Utilize Bank Products
Fully u*tilize bank products and services.*

Article # 7 How Real Women Buy Insurance
Effectively use insurance products as a wealth management tools.

Article # 8 How Real Women Shop for Investment Advice
Get what you need without giving them more than you should.

Article # 9 How Real Women Lay Down Their Own Law
Incorporate legal services efficiently and effectively.

Article # 10 How Real Women Change the World of Finance
Demand what you need from the financial industry.

CHAPTER 11:

Uncle Sam is number one.

Everyone wants an investment advisor to make them 50% on their money risk free, but every American citizen already has a person who can do that for them – their tax advisor.

Your tax advisor should be the first person you go to before you accept a job, negotiate employee benefits, get married, have children, go to the voting polls, start a business, do any home improvement, retire, before you do just about anything, and certainly before you die. Know the tax benefits and implications for everything you intend to do before you do it.

Taking advantage of tax laws and avoiding tax pitfalls can capture or protect a greater percentage of your money than any investment can offer. Tax laws are created to be used by tax payers, but millions of dollars lay unclaimed because people aren't using the tax laws effectively. Retirees who rely on their investment portfolios for retirement income are lying awake at night worrying when their fear could easily be put to rest in a variety of ways using tax laws. Effective wealth management maximizes the benefits of tax laws and the many opportunities they bring.

The two most important aspects of sound wealth management are making money and avoiding taxes. You don't need to be a billionaire to benefit from tax laws or need a tax shelter. Nor do you need to open an account in the Cayman Islands. Tax advisors can help you determine how to benefit from all the tax laws in effect for any given year. Since tax laws change every year on January 1st, you need to meet with your tax advisor in enough time to position yourself before the end of every year. A good tax advisor can help you determine investment strategies and asset placement, harvest capital gains, maximize retirement planning options, and much more.

Effective wealth management maximizes the benefits of tax laws.

While a tax *preparer* knows a lot about taxes and can answer many of your questions, seek a qualified *advisor* with credentials and who is legally able to provide such advice, such as Certified Public Accountants who practice in the area of tax planning.

While some CPAs offer investment services in addition to their tax services, never use your tax advisor as your investment advisor. In my opinion, they make terrible investment advisors. Tax advisors are often licensed only as a Series 6 which limits them to only being able to sell packaged products, such as mutual funds. They offer this more as a convenience to tax clients seeking tax shelters, not as an investment practice. By the very nature of their primary interest – crunching numbers – they tend to be too conservative to offer investment advice. My suggestion is for you to coordinate the advice you receive from your tax advisor with the advice you receive from your investment advisor to maximize the benefits of both.

The government influences you through taxation. Know who is pulling your strings, and why.

Politics is what creates taxes. Your government influences you through taxation. When there is a need to increase the population, you get child deductions. When there is a need to decrease the population, your child deductions are reduced. When the economy needs to be stimulated, you get either deductions or credits for doing specific business transactions – either buying or selling real estate. Business regulation is also influenced by taxation. If you do what we want you to do you get a tax advantage; if not, you don't.

Since our tax structure already supports the vast majority of the needs of our citizens (military, interstate road construction, food and drug regulation, public health issues, etc.) it cannot be altered drastically without causing calamity in all directions. Therefore when a candidate purports to want to lower taxes, he or she is usually referring to capital gains tax – the interest earned on investments, business deals and real estate profits; and estate taxes, which are taxes on the appreciation of assets for which capital gains were not paid prior to death.

Individuals who make more of their money on capital gains versus income from wages stand to benefit more by lowering these taxes. Also, people in line to either inherit or grant estates greater than $5.46 million will benefit from lower estate taxes. Everyone else, however, will either have to cough up more in taxes, or do without or with less of some other public benefit (schools, roads, housing, transportation, veteran's services, etc.) in order to keep the country running smoothly.

People who outlive their money don't need to worry about estate taxes. They need to worry about Human Services being available for them in their final days so they don't wind up on the curb. People who have more than $5.46 million to pass to heirs upon their death don't need to worry about Federal Estate Tax, but a person who dies with $5.47 million does. Before you vote for a candidate because they profess to lower taxes, be certain that it will affect you positively and not negatively. Your tax advisor can tell you how each political platform affects you financially. A really good thing to know before you vote, don't you think?

Tax laws are based on a decision of how much we collect from whom and for what purpose. The various political parties all believe they have the best idea on how to run the country, as a whole, but each party represents the interests of a particular sector of constituents. Its planks are generally based on fiduciary impact of any proposed legislation on that particular demographic. All ideals purported by any political party are mere promotional tactics to earn votes. The bottom line is all about money. It is the only form of communication that works between a government and its constituents.

Similarly, in the home, an 'ideal' is cleanliness and order. You might attempt to promote this by urging a teenager to clean their room, but it is the eminent reward of being paid an allowance or punishment of withholding an opportunity that gets the job done. The same tactics are used on taxpayers.

Since we are a country of many states (the United States), you need to keep in mind that each state has its own tax laws that can differ from state to state. Depending on which state you die in, you may or may not need to worry about estate taxes. To find out whether you need to consider estate taxation, see your tax advisor *and* your legal advisor if you spend any significant amount of time outside your resident state. It is essential to sound wealth management to coordinate tax advice with legal advice relative to all states and countries in which you hold any interests, including travel plans, time-shares, potential heirs or benefactors, real estate, business interests, etc.

There are no right or wrong answers to tax concerns. Tax laws affect everyone, and unless you know how they affect your household, you cannot vote according to your best interests. Educate yourself about local, state and federal tax laws and how they affect your household before you vote.

Vote according to your best interests.

It is not wrong to run on any issue that wins you a vote. As a voter, however, you need to know the facts and not be swayed by propaganda that could harm you financially. Should you decide to vote against your own best interests, you ought to know that you are doing so at the time you vote, rather than be blind-sided later.

The gift tax is another tax which can affect the wealthy. You can gift up to $14,000 to as many people as you want each year without having to pay a gift tax. Millions of dollars are transferred in this fashion TAX FREE every year. The more you have to gift, the more important this tax break is to you.

On the other hand, the more wealth that is transferred in this fashion, the less tax revenue there is to pay for government programs that you may be counting upon.

If your net worth is over $5 million and/or your income is higher than $450,000, or you make most of your money on capital gains, or you stand to inherit more than $5 million, you want to vote for candidates who will help create the tax codes that will benefit you: lower capital gains and inheritance taxes, more business deductions, less regulation. Your choice will likely be for a Republican.

If your net worth is less than $5 million and/or your income is less than $450,000 per year and you don't have a chance of inheriting more than $5 million, you want to vote for candidates who will help create the tax codes that will benefit you: marital deductions, healthcare deductions, child deductions, small business tax credits and deductions, whatever helps you maintain your lifestyle. Even though some regulations may impact you, more often than not you will benefit from more regulations on big business because regulation protects lesser beings from the powerful ones. Finally, you need to ask yourself whether or not you can live without Social Security benefits – while you also consider the needs of others who you feel responsible for, such as aging parents – could they live without Social Security? Are you willing to help your loved ones financially, or would you prefer that your government does? If you fall into this category, you will likely choose a Democrat.

All political parties will campaign on any issue that might win votes, and there is nothing wrong with that. We live in a free country where you can purport anything you wish – true or not. However, once in office, they will lean toward their party platform in supporting legislation which affects either the ultra-wealthy or the extremely poor. It is your job to know where you fall in between, know how much you are willing to sacrifice for the good of all mankind, and to prepare yourself accordingly for whichever party is in office.

It is sound wealth management to know how each candidate will affect you. You cannot obtain such information through Facebook or Twitter, or even your friends. You must research each candidate's platform and the platform of the political party that endorses them. There you will find written statements to which their constituents and the free press will hold these candidates accountable. All other claims during a campaign are mere tactics and propaganda to gain votes and should _not_ be considered factual.

Tax laws are your greatest financial resource. No Wall Street firm can offer anything that compares to the advantages that tax laws offer. Sound wealth management maximizes tax opportunities.

To learn how tax laws can benefit you financially, see a qualified Certified Public Accountant (CPA).

See _ARTICLE #5: How Real Women Treat Tax Laws_
at www.RealWomenManageWealth.com

CHAPTER 12:

Lay down your own law.

Legal advice is essential to sound wealth management, but the biggest mistake people make is to go to estate planning attorneys prematurely. Before you seek legal advice, explore all the other possibilities. By the time you seek legal advice you should already know what you need from them.

While attorneys can provide solutions for many financial concerns by creating legal documents, those solutions are not always the best, most cost efficient, or simplest ways to do so. You should also know that an attorney is not apprised, nor qualified to advise you about anything outside legal documents and proceedings. Each of the five areas of finance require specific licensing, training, and expertise beyond what is taught in law school.

There are many ways to address any financial concern. Investigate all the other options with your other advisors (banker, insurance agent, investment advisor, tax advisor) before seeing an estate attorney. By knowing all the other possibilities, you will better coordinate the advice an attorney offers.

Estate attorneys sell personalized legal documents. They are wills, health directives, guardianships, trusts, powers of attorney, and more. The law is complicated, which is why you need a qualified lawyer, even if it is only to bless the other potential solutions you are considering. Even if you solve your concern by using any one of the other areas, it would be wise to have a qualified attorney look over your intentions to be certain your choice is the right one given the laws of the state in which you reside.

Because we live in the United States, laws differ between the states, so you may need to see a qualified attorney in every state in which you have financial interests, hold real estate, or in which you spend a significant amount of time. A qualified estate attorney in your area can determine whether, or not, you have additional needs outside their jurisdiction.

Most people want to transfer wealth to heirs, reduce estate taxes, and protect their wealth from being spent entirely on healthcare in their later years. Most people want to leave something to loved ones. Some people are concerned about privacy and want to avoid probate, which requires assets be made public. All these issues can be addressed in a variety of ways, using everything from banking services, insurance products, investment accounts, and tax laws, in addition to legal documents. However, before making any decision, you should have a qualified attorney examine your situation to make certain it is the right choice under the law.

Hiding assets from a nursing home could put both you and your attorney in jail.

Sometimes people want to hide assets from a nursing home, but that's a big no-no. Hiding assets from a nursing home is illegal and both you and your attorney could go to jail. However, a certified elder law attorney can assist you in positioning yourself within the law to take advantage of government programs and laws which were meant to assist you and your loved ones legally. If your aging parent, or you, are concerned about the cost of health care eating up all your assets, see an attorney with expertise in elder law.

Things everyone ought to know:

- Health directives, or living wills, instruct the doctors as to how you wish to be treated if you are unable to tell them yourself.
- Wills designate who gets your stuff after you die.
- Durable Powers of Attorney gives someone else temporary permission to take care of your business in the event that you are temporarily unable.
- Guardianships guarantee that your children will be placed into loving arms immediately – versus them going to strangers as foster children.

Families who grow up playing with one another, who gather around the same Thanksgiving Day table, who you hope will be there for one another throughout life, are torn apart every single day for one reason: one or both of their parents die without a will. Civil war is a terrible thing to witness, especially when it is between your own family members.

Family discord as a result of benefactors dying without a will is spawning big business.

Discord among heirs is big business. Not only for lawyers, but also for psychologists, psychiatrists, and family counselors who have developed specialized practices devoted to nothing but families who contest wills or who are at odds with one another due to the lack of one. These services are prominent businesses in the financial industry today which shows how common it is for heirs to squabble. If you do not wish to support the destruction of your family, get a will!

Never assume your children will do right by you, by each other, or even for themselves. What you do, or don't do, will result as your legacy. What do you want to leave behind? Love or discord? Very few conflicts arise when something is declared in writing as a person's last will and testament – even when a rightful heir is purposely excluded. While someone might be mad, they will be mad at you, not the family members still alive. Let your legacy be to keep those you love together, continuing to be part of each other's lives.

Now for my little rant: the biggest swindle currently occurring within the legal arena is selling unnecessary trusts. Each year, consumers lose hundreds and thousands of dollars through the purchase of living trusts which are unnecessary and can even leave consumers with greater problems affiliated with the trust. While there are valid reasons for having a trust, less than 10-percent of US households might actually need them, according to 2010 census data. Selling trusts, however, has turned into a billion-dollar business. Attorneys are drafting them left and right because they are finding it easy business to sell someone on the benefits of a trust and there is nothing stopping them from doing so – no regulation or laws which requires full disclosure. Based on this one aspect, it could be said that the advice lawyers give about trusts is more incorrect than correct and is inconsistent with the needs of consumers.

Most trusts created are worthless and unnecessary.

So how will you know whether a trust is in your best interest or the best interest of the lawyer selling it? Well, for certain you will never find the answer at any free meal or community education class that purports to educate the public about the benefits of estate planning. It is impossible to learn anything meaningful to your situation in two hours or less. Eat the meal, but do not leave your contact information or see these people again for any reason. They've already proved they are untrustworthy. This is not the approach reputable legal advisors take to build their business, although it is very typical of investment advisors to pair with lawyers just to lure people to topics which appeal to people with significant wealth, such as estate planning, tax planning, and charitable giving.

While few people are as willing to attend a dinner where stocks are being promoted, many are more than willing to attend anything where they think they might learn how to do something smart with their wealth. The smartest thing you can do is to never attend any such event. You cannot learn anything meaningful to your situation in two hours or less.

These types of marketing tactics are widely used in the financial industry. It is a way for investment advisors to wind up with a room full of quality leads. This is their chance to warm you up with their generosity and their sparkling demeanor, before they walk away with your name and contact information. Chances are you aren't going to be as rude to someone who gave you a meal, or whose hand you shook, as you would with a typical cold call. Bingo. They gotcha.

The benefit of an attorney to pair with an investment advisor is they get to sell trusts to a roomful of prospects versus one at a time, while someone else picks up the tab. Such events cost money, which makes rookie lawyers and rookie accountants sitting ducks for aggressive rookie stock brokers who are backed by their firms with more marketing tactics and money than you can shack a stick at. These events are not public service events. They are sales events.

If you haven't gotten an invitation to a free dinner to hear a qualified attorney talk about estate planning, you will before you turn 65. Don't go. They are sales traps. Most people pay dearly in the long run for eating a free meal.

It is impossible to learn anything meaningful at a free seminar or meal.

By learning more about what you need and don't need you are better able to avoid paying thousands of dollars for a trust you don't need and will never use; or worse, wind up with a legal noose around your neck for reasons you should have avoided. Meet with all five types of financial professionals regarding the same concern to discover all possible solutions before you buy a trust.

There are some excellent reasons why a person might need a trust, however. To name a few:

1. If you own property in another state,
2. If you are concerned that you might become disabled and that as a result you will be subject to undue influence,
3. If beneficiaries of your estate are disabled,
4. If you live or spend a significant amount of time in a state in which probate is time-consuming, burdensome and costly.

Make certain, however, there are no better solutions to your situation than a trust before you buy one.

A few more things you should know about living revocable trusts:

- They are much more expensive to set up and maintain than a will.
- Keeping things inside and outside your trust defeats the primary benefits of owning a trust.
- Probate can be avoided in other ways: transfer on death deeds, beneficiary designations, holding assets jointly, etc.
- They do not protect your assets from creditors and lawsuits.
- Revocable trusts can adversely affect your eligibility for Medicaid nursing home benefits.
- They are no more effective than wills in saving state and federal estate taxes.
- A revocable trust is useless as a 'Medicaid asset transfer' no matter when it is created.
- Living trusts can and are contested, just like a will.
- Administering a living trust after your death is not cost-free
- After your death, your living trust will not cut off the claims of your creditors against the trust corpus. Often a trustee will need to open a probate estate anyway.

Lawyers give out advice, but there is evidence that they don't always give out the best advice. Protect yourself from poor legal advice:

- Question everything you are told, especially about living trusts.

- Beware of anyone trying to sell you financial products in addition to a living trust, or any other legal product. This is a clear sign there are ulterior motives involved that are likely not in your best interest.
- Get a second or even third professional opinion, particularly on whether a living trust is right for you.

Keep legal advice relative to your wealth in perspective.

DISCLOSURE: THIS SEGMENT IS NOT MEANT TO GIVE LEGAL ADVICE. You are not to rely on the limited information given here. Before acting on any information presented in this book, you are strongly urged to consult with an attorney who is competent in estate law, elder law, or any other type of legal advice that is required.

CHAPTER 13:

Beware of wolves in sheep's clothing.

The financial industry is the only industry which purports false credentials and gets away with it. The titles on business cards, particularly in the investment industry, are devised for the purpose of convincing prospects of an impressive range of expertise which rarely is provided. The reason for this is to more quickly earn your trust so they can get at your money. They do it because they can and because it works.

No one is more capable of managing your wealth than you. You are the only person you can trust with this resource for two reasons:

> 1) you are the only person who knows why you need money; and

> 2) you are the only person who cares enough to make certain it is used appropriately to your needs.

Everyone else in the world is going to pull you away from what you want in order to get what *they* want. Most of all, financial advisors: the very people you want so much to rely upon. No matter how much you *want* to believe they are sincere about helping you maintain and attain more wealth, don't you believe it for one minute. Financial advisors are salespeople who are more interested in making their boat and mortgage payments than helping you make yours. Never forget that.

I know it is hard to think of all those nice, clean people in starched shirts with impeccable manners as being anything but the kindest, most helpful people you can possibly imagine, but that's exactly what they want you to believe. A financial advisor's objective is to make as much money as possible using your money without going to jail. Some succeed at doing so, and others go to jail. However, anyone would be a fool if they are gullible enough to believe there are a bunch of good people just waiting to help them manage their wealth.

The employment model within the financial industry is based on results – assets brought into the firm. Some of the highest commissions in the world are possible, and firms paint a pretty picture for anyone interested in making big bucks without getting their hands dirty. That said, similar to casinos, financial firms are set up so the house always wins. Firms precariously dangle gold rings to get their advisors to do anything to grab them (since the advisors are the ones who pay the fines and go to jail).

When an advisor fails, they leave all their assets on the table, since the firm is the actual owner of them. The fat cats divide up the spoils and the game goes on. If you are one of the fat cats, you aren't about to tell anyone how you are getting rich. And if you lose the game for any reason, you are too embarrassed to admit that to anyone. There is honor among pirates.

At a casino, the house always wins.

Why is this important for you to know? Well, imagine if your medical doctor were required to perform a certain number of surgeries every month in order to keep their job. Wouldn't you want to know that before they schedule you to have your gallbladder taken out as a precaution?

What makes women more vulnerable is their innate tendencies to create meaningful relationships with everyone in their life. While this is an admirable character trait, it is the very thing which breaks down the barrier one ought to have between themselves and their financial advisors. With something as important as your money – which is your primary resource for everything you need in life – it is imperative you maintain a cautious distance from all financial advisors. Keep a critical eye and a cynical mind at all times. Gestures of kindness from any financial professional should be considered no different than candy being offered to children. Sometimes the intent is sincere and harmless. And sometimes it is not.

Maintain a cautious distance from all financial advisors.

Another reason women are more vulnerable is the entire female culture is void of money talk. Women grow up with far less exposure to money matters than males get from male culture. As a result, women are more easily overwhelmed to the point they want to throw up their hands and turn over decisions to someone else. For all the reasons I've been pointing out throughout this book, women are at a disadvantage in acquiring financial advice due to gender-specific traits, personal experiences, social expectations and norms that they've adapted to, and the current financial environment, which is not conducive for women. For all these reasons and more, women face a tremendous challenge in trying to manage their wealth effectively and efficiently, and now I have to add one more thing to that list: false titles and credentials.

The financial industry is notorious for creating impressive titles which require no expertise and sometimes no experience to bear. In all other industries, a professional title implies an area of expertise: Hospital Administrator, Dean of Academics, Vice President of a company, Information Technology Specialist, Professor, Sales Executive. However, in the financial industry, titles are created for the sole purpose of exaggerating expertise and promoting confidence to lure unsuspecting prospects and clients. This includes titles such as: Financial Advisor, Financial Specialist, Retirement Specialist, Senior Retirement Specialist, Vice President of Investments, Vice President of Retirement Planning, Financial Planner, Certified Financial Planner, Chartered Insurance

Underwriter, and many, many more. This often leads a person to expect more expertise than the bearer is willing to provide. As we breathe, additional titles are being contrived for one purpose – to fool you.

It requires a lot of study, passing of exams, licensing requirements, and continuing education to become a financial expert in any one of the five areas of finance. However, there are no requirements for anyone who achieves such credentials to actually perform according to any of the credentials they purport. Basically, these financial advisors are no different than a gynecologist who makes diagnosis without ever doing a pap test or breast exam.

It sounds unethical, and it is, but it is within the law and regulations at this time, therefore, it has become the financial industry norm for financial advisors to purport to be something they are not.

Financial advisors purport to be something they are not.

Well. If you are like all the other women I've mentored over the years, this news is about as devastating as learning your lover is cheating on you. Imagine your daughter, sister, or best friend is dating a person you know to be unscrupulous. Would you not want to warn her even though it could dash her expectations and destroy her dreams? My intent for you is that you find true happiness by entering into relationships with financial advisors with caution, and maintaining control over the relationship at all times. This is not a place where you should be cooperative and nice.

Women tend to cling to their financial advisors like long lost lovers. If there is one thing which women particularly need to remember, it is this: no matter how endearing a financial advisor presents themselves, they are salespeople working to close a sale. While it is okay to enter into such relationships, do so as the person in charge, not as the pawn.

Once an advisor has your trust, they do as little as possible to keep you happy, which makes them happiest.

One of the most misused titles is the Certified Financial Planner (CFP). The title implies that the bearer is capable of conducting a complete financial assessment for the purpose of providing specific advice to a specific person or household. Since that's what we all want from any financial advisor, it is understandable that such credentials would impress us. However, it takes days and often weeks to conduct such an investigation, and no one should be expected to do so without reasonable compensation. Typically, a suitable client for a legitimate financial planner should expect to pays 1% of the assets being assessed. It doesn't begin to pencil out until there is a minimum of $1 million, but more likely over $3 million in assets – and even then it may not be worth what it costs. A formal agreement is entered into prior to such services. If you aren't required to sign such, nor expected to pay a fee well into the thousands for a one-time piece of advice to someone touting such credentials, don't expect anything more than a sales pitch.

The primary reason most of the financial professionals who carry such credentials do not actually apply their knowledge is for the simple reason they don't need to. Most people do not realize what it takes to actually perform any of the tasks associated with any of the credentials listed on most business cards, so no one is the wiser. It is no secret among advisors who continue to collect as many credentials as possible with no intention of performing in any particular capacity other than sales.

If everyone hosting such credentials actually performed the duties expected of them, there might never have been a global financial collapse of 2008, or any other time. After the crash, investors were told by their advisors that the markets are unpredictable. If that were really true, no one would need an advisor, would they?

I stood on the deck of the ship when it went down in 2008, but neither myself nor any of my clients who took my advice lost a dime in that financial disaster. While I didn't know what was causing the rumbling and the shaking at the time, as a financial advisor I felt it was my job to identify when the rumbling and the shaking was cause for concern. I advised my clients accordingly (which is different for each person, by the way) and within a short time had them all prepared for the inevitable. If I could do that, every other advisor could have done that, too. Did yours? I'm not bragging, but rather trying to show you what to expect from a proper advisor.

People pull you away from what you want to get what they want.

There are hard-working, honest financial advisors out there, but finding them requires a lot of due diligence on your part. Vet each of your advisors thoroughly, and hold them accountable to consistently prove the value of their service to you. Go find friends elsewhere in your life, if you want a trustworthy relationship. Never befriend a financial advisor to the point you no longer question their advice, unless they pay your mortgage for you.

Good advisors understand the complexities of the marketplace. One right for you will align with your tolerance for risk. If you are not willing to suffer market collapses and bubbles, then choose an advisor who will actually advise you on avoiding them while still helping you invest. A good advisor should be flexible for all types of investors.

This entire chapter was meant to scare you to the point you trust no one in the financial industry. The very nature of the financial industry attracts people interested in making money. Therefore, you should always assume that every financial professional has more interest in the money they can make selling you their products and/or services than in helping you. While there are truly honorable financial professionals, there is no way for you to ever know for certain whether you've found one. Therefore, my advice stands. Trust no one in the financial industry to help you more than they will help themselves.

Use financial advisors strictly as research tools. Allow them to inform, educate, and show you what you need to know. In the end, you must take full responsibility for every decision you make. Until you understand what they are telling you and see for yourself the benefits of whatever they suggest, and feel absolutely comfortable with every decision you make, you need to keep asking questions. You are already wired to make good decisions for yourself, but because you are a female you need all the facts before you are ready to make a decision. Do not allow your confidence in someone else to make financial decisions on your behalf. Only you will reap the reward or pay the price for your decisions.

Ignorance and indecision makes you a sitting duck for any financial advisor.

Remember, the entire financial world is geared for males who do not require as much time to make a buying decision. Since females typically require more information and more time to contemplate before they are comfortable making a buying decision, you must stand your ground against sales pressure until you feel ready to make the best decision. Women who take their time shopping for advice make better decisions and outperform males, according to several studies. So, take your time.

Always know how your financial advisor is compensated. The more you know about how they benefit from your business, the better you can protect your interests. I mean to scare you, because there are more wolves in sheep's clothing in the financial world than underground drug smuggling. The more convincing a financial professional is in making you feel comfortable and confident in their intentions is only a demonstration of their ability to deceive. Do not be deceived. If you feel comfortable and confident, be sure that comes from your understanding of the product or service, not from trust in your advisor. Demand to be fully educated about every product or service they offer, *and* demand ample time for you to digest information and make the right decision for yourself. Never allow yourself to be talked into anything you do not fully understand.

The financial industry is void of virtue.

Unlike any other industry in which there is an element of virtue, in the financial industry there is none. Even if there are a few people out there with honorable intent to help others, my suggestion still stands. You will be better off trusting no one than believing you have found one that is truly trustworthy, because there is no way you will ever really know.

Financial professionals eventually wind up justifying their roles as essential to mankind, but the truth of the matter is they benefit themselves more than anyone else by being a financial advisor. I hate to sound like a naysayer, but my purpose for writing this book is to help women. If there is one piece of advice that will help women the most, it is this: do not trust your financial advisors. Period.

CHAPTER 14:
Shop like your life depends on it, because it does.

Managing your wealth is no different than managing your wardrobe. When you need something, you shop for just the right thing. It is the same when shopping for financial solutions to all your goals.

The financial world changes constantly. Not only is it impossible for any one person to know all there is to know about all five areas of wealth management, but it is impossible to keep up with the constant changes in each of these areas. That being the case, there is no one person who is capable of providing you all the advice you need. What you need is a plethora of advice from several different sources.

Would you go to one store, look at one item of clothing and buy it without looking around? Of course not. The same holds true for making decisions about your money. Shop around. Compare. Use the same tactics you use when you shop for anything else.

You will know what is best when you find it. While your mother once picked out all your clothing, don't you do a better job yourself? You are the only one who knows what your money needs to do for you. Not your mate, not your mother, not your father, not your children, definitely not your financial advisors – all they can do is help you gather the facts you need to make a good decision. They can't make the decisions for you unless you let them.

Use financial advisors exactly like store clerks. Allow them to lead you to items which may be suitable, but you are the only one who can make the decision for yourself.

Your life is a reflection of your decisions. Manage your resources (time, talents, and money) appropriate to your desires.

The five basic areas of finance in which you need to shop are:

- Banking
- Insurance
- Investments
- Taxes
- Law

As a consumer you need to understand that the advice you receive from any financial professional is limited to their area of expertise by law, and limited to the products and services offered by their firm, which they are obligated to promote.

What does this mean for you? It means you can't go to just one financial professional (banker, insurance agent, investment advisor, tax advisor, or lawyer) and expect to get all the answers. It means that no one person can give you all the answers. It also means you need to meet with representatives from all five areas to learn what each can do for you in every circumstance.

All five areas offer solutions that may be suitable to any particular financial need or concern, but not always the best solutions for *every* situation. If you go only to one advisor, you are likely to get a limited answer. By going to representatives in all five areas you will eventually expand your knowledge while limiting everything there is to know to just the things *you* need to know. By asking the same questions from each advisor, you will soon realize just how vast your options are.

Shop like a woman.

Your personalized list of goals should be conveyed in part or in whole to representatives from each of the five areas. As an example: when you ask an expert how they can help you become financially secure for the rest of your life instead of asking them what you should do to prepare for retirement you will get a whole different conversation – one that is specific to your needs.

Bring your notebook in which you've written out all your goals. Go through your list, share your concerns, your fears and expectations. Sounds simple, but this will likely be the thing you will try to avoid doing most. Don't skip this step. It is what differentiates it from all other methods of wealth management, and it is the step which will bring women the most success. Once you get the hang of it, it will come as easily to you as shopping for anything else.

Shopping for financial solutions to your concerns can be exciting and fun. Invite your friends, go as a group and include lunch. Just because it hasn't been done that way doesn't mean it shouldn't be done that way. Malls wouldn't exist if women still bought material and patterns from the general store. Step into the future. This is your time to show the entire financial industry how you want to shop for their products and services.

Make a shopping list before shopping for financial advice.

So what should you include on your shopping list? Anything and everything important to you. Rather than clump all your objectives into one goal, such as saving for retirement, my suggestion is to separate your financial objectives and/or concerns and shop for solutions to each independently, such as wanting to make certain you never run out of money before you die. With each type of advisor address each of your goals and/or concerns individually. Take notes as to the suggestions they offer.

Here are a few things you might want to include on your list of financial products and services to shop for:

EXAMPLE: If you are concerned that you will outlive your money either because of longevity or a health cost, your shopping list should include things like:

- Proof that you won't outlive your money for any reason
- Peace of mind (this should always be on every list because what is the point of finding a solution if it doesn't keep your head on the pillow?)

Since this is all about managing money wisely, your list should also include things like:

- Cost efficient

And since it is your list and no one else's, you can add things like:

- Easy to understand
- Simple to manage

or, if you feel up to more challenge, ask for:

- Highly complicated and state-of-the-art solutions
- Solutions which require constant professional management

Anything you desire in a remedy which addresses your concern or goal should be on your shopping list. Your list should represent your goals, desires, concerns and fears about wealth management.

When your list is ready, so are you. Take it with you and rattle it off to every type of financial professional: banker, insurance agent, investment advisor, tax advisor and lawyer. Be sure to bring along a notepad and pencil to take notes on what each person tells you. You will need all that information to compare their answers and eventually make your decision.

Do not buy anything from anyone at this time. You are merely window shopping for advice, not buying.

Women typically need financial solutions to more objectives than currently offered by the financial industry, which focuses primarily on:

- college funding for children
- retirement
- healthcare costs

While these may still be included in what women want and need, there are so many more things women are concerned about which don't fit into one of these three plans, such as:

- Finding time, energy, and resources to fulfill their personal life's dream
- Making a difference in the lives of others, charitable contributions, foundations, and other humanitarian interests fulfilled
- Making sure their kids don't gobble up every dime before they leave home
- Ensuring that their spouse doesn't run off with some tart and leave them hanging
- A number of other things which women worry about

No matter what you want to do, there is a way to do it. Know what you are looking for, then go ask every type of financial expert how they might help you reach total peace of mind about each of those issues. It takes no more time to shop for financial advice than a wedding dress...but it is far more important to your happiness.

No matter what your situation or concern, there is always a solution.

Gender differences play a larger role than most women want to believe. I would urge every woman to review Chapter 2 prior to meeting with any financial professional. Become cognizant of gender differences both in the way others react to you and how you respond to them.

What rules have you created for yourself that will prevent you from acquiescing to gender traits which could work against your best interest? Remember what 'feels' right isn't always right. What criteria will you use to determine whether something is suitable for you? While relying on your gut instincts and intuition is advisable in most instances involving money, it is not advisable when selecting financial advisors of any type for two reasons:

1. All financial professionals are trained to sell themselves first, to establish trust, to create a bond with a prospective client and they are very good at it.
2. As a woman, you instinctively have a tendency to form a good relationship with everyone, particularly people who portray a genuine interest in you (which every financial professional is likely to do).

These two things do not work in a female's favor when it comes to locating sound advice. While I cannot tell you why women act differently toward wealth advisors than males, my decades of personal experience advising women attest to the fact they do. Therefore, as a woman, you must be aware of your vulnerabilities and prepare yourself appropriately prior to meeting with any financial professional.

Go to more than one professional in each category because firms differ in the types of service and/or products they offer. The more information you acquire, the easier it will be for you to make the right decision. Much can be accomplished by phone calls.

If you are concerned about racking up a bill in the process of obtaining information from certain professionals, negotiate fees prior to any meeting. Most professionals won't charge for informational meetings.

The following examples illustrate how to create a question from some of the typical concerns women share:

EXAMPLE 1: If you desire to feel financially secure, you should ask the question "How can your products and/or services make me feel financially secure?"

EXAMPLE 2: If you are concerned that your spouse will squander all your hard-earned money and thereby thwart all hope of retiring, you should ask the question "How can you help me prevent my husband from squandering my money so I can retire someday?"

EXAMPLE 3: Even though you are currently financially sound, if you worry that you will outlive your money, you should ask: "How can you help me feel confident that I won't outlive my money?"

EXAMPLE 4: Should you have a concern about keeping peace among your family on account of a particular situation which involves money, inheritance or financial obligations, you should ask: "How might you help me solve this particular situation," and explain the situation.

EXAMPLE 5: If you want to retire someday, you need to know how much your desired retirement lifestyle will cost before you make any plan toward achieving it. Your questions should convey some particulars about how, when and where you intend to retire so your financial advisors can calculate realistically. Your questions should be something like: "How can you help me retire at age 62 and afford a lifestyle which costs $80,000 a year in today's dollars for about 40 years?" The advice you receive should walk you through a maze of things which need to be achieved before anyone can give you a good answer to that, but none-the-less your questions should be something of that sort.

EXAMPLE 6: if you desire the best for your newborn baby, and are certain your child will go to college someday, your questions should be: "How can you help me prepare financially for my child's college education?" But if you are uncertain about your child attending college, or wish to let your child have more control over their future, your questions should be something like: "How can you help me plan for my child's future, not knowing what that future holds?"

Crafting the proper questions to ask professionals is a matter of being able to convey the situation or concern as honestly and clearly as possible. Finding the best solution for your situation is a matter of asking that same question to enough financial professionals.

Ask various financial advisors the same <u>exact</u> question to best compare.

Once you acquire a sufficient amount of information and have had time to contemplate a decision in the privacy of your own home, then (and only then) are you ready to go back to any particular financial advisor with your decision. The ball is now in your court. When you identify the product or service right for you, it is up to you to manage the advisor who can facilitate it or supply it to you. Not the other way around.

At no time is it wise to commission anyone who you would find difficult to fire. Let that be one of your requirements for hiring any type of financial advisor in the first place. You should be willing and able to fire any one of your advisors who fails you at any time and replace them with someone who serves you better. This one rule can be more valuable to you than any single piece of advice any one advisor may give you. Sometimes the best way to manage your wealth is to fire your wealth manager and find a new one.

Before you begin to shop for financial advice be prepared to convey your current financial situation. This means having a general, but good, idea of your current household net worth, income, and expenses. Good financial advice helps people get from one point to another. Therefore, advisors need to know the starting point before they can make suitable suggestions.

When you meet with any type of financial professional, always expect to be informed, but never buy on the first meeting.

Know that professionals keep records of what is said during all meetings to protect themselves and their firms from lawsuits. You should do the same.

At a minimum take notes as to the date, time of day, name of the advisor and the firm, and topics discussed, plus anything else which seems important.

There are many solutions to every financial concern, goal, or situation. There is only one way to discover what they all might be: shop, shop, shop. This is where women shine above men. They take more time to compare, consider more thoroughly, and as a result more often make better decisions as scientific studies prove.

Always shop all five areas of finance when shopping for any type of advice.

While women tend to be better shoppers, they also have a tendency to want to create meaningful relationships where they shouldn't. If you ever find yourself thinking you really trust and like your financial advisor, take a step back and review everything I just told you about all financial advisors—even if they are your best friends, relatives, or your own child.

To be blind to the roles financial professionals play in your life is to put yourself in harm's way.

Women are at risk of bonding with abandon when anyone seems willing to spare them from having to do anything with icky drains, bugs, rodents, and wealth management. Don't be afraid to do your own dirty work when it comes to wealth management.

Select your advisors based on the type of firm they represent, and their ability to educate you about the products and services they represent without pressuring you for a decision. Meet with representatives from all five areas, and from more than one firm of the same type, even interview multiple people within the same firm. Then, compare what you learned about them all before you make your decision about which person to use as your advisor.

Feel free to ask as many questions as you want, but here are a few questions to ask any financial professional:

1. What can your firm offer me in the way of products and services?
2. What is the cost of your products and services?
3. How do you get paid?
4. What are your credentials and experience?
5. Who is your competition? Why are you better than your competition?

While you do not need to become a financial expert yourself, or even know much at all about any particular area of finance, you need to learn to effectively and efficiently coordinate the products and services that these experts offer or they will be useless to you, even harmful. Shopping will educate you about everything you will ever need to know.

Shopping for financial advice should be a learning experience, <u>not</u> a buying experience.

CHAPTER 15:
Say it like you mean it.

Neuroscience now has proof that the left-right, and front-back brain dichotomies actually respond differently in men than women. They are not telling us anything new, but the whole perspective changes as a result of such scientific data. We can stop thinking anything will change. It won't. However, instead of feeling hopeless, this actually offers legitimate hope because now, at least, we know what we are dealing with.

Effective communication is essential to sound wealth management. Your financial success depends on your ability to effectively communicate with every person who affects your financial stability, such as:

- Your spouse, or mate
- Your children
- Your parents
- Your siblings
- Your professional advisors

So, how do you know whether there is a communication barrier or whether you are just talking to the wall?

Let's start with the fun part – talking money with our honey. Three out of ten married couples argue about finances at least once a month, according to Marriage Partnership research. How have those discussions been going so far for you? Would you say each of you are making your point with the other? Would you say your discussions have been mutually engaging, or are they a little one-sided? Do either of you feel as though they are being poked with a stick? Are declarations of war, truce agreements, and instruments of surrender part of your money discussions? Unfortunately, many women find themselves in these positions. If you are one of them, or if your situation includes a guy who won't listen to anything you say, do not expect anything to change unless you are willing to change yourself.

If you are not one who has difficulty communicating with their significant other about money be sympathetic to the many women who still do. They could be your mothers, grandmothers, aunts, some friends and neighbors. They need your compassion and understanding. You need to be aware of the world around you. If you care about these women, you need to help them with what you know about effective communication.

Regardless of whether there is a communication problem, we all can improve communication with our mates.

Three out of ten married couples argue about finances at least once a month

Remember the chapter on money attitude? We learned how society has shaped our thinking. The way in which we communicate has also been shaped by society. Combined with social factors here in the United States, what science has learned is that during adolescence girls tend to minimize *themselves* as a means to better understand *others*; while boys tend to minimize *others* to better understand *themselves*.

As a result, boys develop a rights based mentality —"What's in it for me?"— while girls develop an ethic-, or responsibility-based mentality – "How will it affect everyone?"

Gender differences exist. The more aware of them you become, the better communicator you will be.

See *ARTICLE #2: How Real Women Adapt Gender Differences* at www.RealWomenManageWealth.com

What are some of the gender differences between men and women?

- Women tend to be contextual. Men tend to be literal.

  o She suggests, but he does not get the hint. He must be told.

  o She says: "I shouldn't have to tell you how to please me. If you loved me, you would know."

  o He says: "I'm not a mind-reader."

- Women strive for closeness, togetherness, a holistic union. Men strive to remain separate, as an individual, and almost fear being swallowed up by anyone else.

  o He says: "You're trying to control me."

  o She says: "No I'm not, I'm trying to bring us closer."

  o He sees her desire to be closer as a direct threat to his individuality.

  o She sees his reluctance to be closer as a direct threat to their relationship.

- She is communal; power among people should be equal. He is hierarchical, always focused on the order of power in all circumstances, particularly among other men and always respects the order. Women will quickly put another woman in her place if she dares to get out of line.

  o She says she wants to share in financial responsibilities.

- He takes that to mean he isn't doing a good enough job in her eyes.

- She is cooperative, while he is competitive. Ever feel as though you argue about the same thing all the time? It might just be that winning the argument is more important to him than finding an agreeable solution. This is a gender trait, not a conscious objection.

  - She says: "I handle money just as well as you."

  - He says: "No you don't."

- She is more comfortable with emotions; he is more comfortable with physical action.

  - She says: "Make me feel loved."

  - He Says: "Anytime, anywhere, anyplace, baby."

There is a lot about human nature which goes back farther than the cave-dwellers. If nothing has changed much since then, don't expect much to change any time soon. However, modern science provides us with a few tips on how to better communicate with one another.

If you want to be a more effective communicator with a male,

- Sit shoulder-to-shoulder, never face-to-face.
- Be verbally concise and to-the-point. Never hint, suggest, or insinuate.
- Positive signs that a man is cooperating with you are:
  - If he turns his back while you are still talking
  - If he breaks eye-contact with you
  - If he puts up any sort of barrier, a newspaper, turns on the television, watches a ballgame, etc.

These are all good signs that he trusts you, has no real objections to what you are saying and wishes you would stop talking. By learning to effectively interpret how males respond, you will be better able to identify when you've made your point, when he is supportive of your ideas, and when you have effectively communicated.

The communication barriers between men and women are natural.

By insisting that he communicate like a female, you are just asking for trouble. He's a guy. Guys communicate differently than gals, and you would no more want to be forced to communicate their way than they do yours.

Why do you have to be the one who adapts to him? Simply because it benefits you to do so. That's it. If you can't effectively communicate your needs to any guy who has influence over your money, then you lose.

The communication barriers between men and women are natural. We don't want to erase them altogether and become genderless. What we want is for the two genders to better understand one another for a common good.

In this case, since communication benefits you more than any other person, particularly any man in your life, it is your responsibility to learn to effectively communicate with *them* – not the other way around.

Before you attempt to communicate with anyone assess your situation. Are you in a good spot, or a bad one? If you are in a good spot, how can it become a better spot? If you already have good communication with your mate, how might it improve knowing what you now know about the differences between the genders? If you are in a bad spot, what exactly needs to change? Are your differences as a result of gender, or are they legitimate personal differences?

Too often couples argue incorrectly over money issues because they assume typical gender-specific postures and respond in typical gender-specific responses. Since this is a course about how women can effectively manage their wealth, it is up to you to figure out how to effectively communicate with your mate. Your wealth is your responsibility, and this responsibility begins with you being able to objectively assess how others interact with you…not the other way around. It is not about being right or wrong. It is about communicating, understanding, and managing effectively.

Some women choose to stay in relationships which are detrimental to their financial stability, but a woman who can anticipate the downside of doing so is far better able to provide a back-up plan for herself than one who is oblivious to her situation.

Realizing you are in a bad spot is the first step to making it better.

I had a client who was married to a wheeler-dealer. He was always making deals that were going to make them millions. Early in their marriage, she drew the line in the sand. He could never use their house as collateral, and she was going to keep her job that offered a good pension. When it came for them to retire, he still hadn't made any good business deals, had spent nearly every dime they made – which was a lot – and had not a penny put aside for his retirement other than a stipend offered by a labor union. She had her house and her pension, and it is enough for the both of them. Together, they created a good marriage, despite the differences in the way each managed money.

Suitable solutions can be created for every situation. Do not despair if your situation isn't perfect. Nobody's is.

Prior to communicating with your mate, identify potential resources which can help. It might be as simple as reading a self-help book or articles online. Find out what other people have done in similar situations, what experts suggest, or see your religious leader or a marriage counselor. Prepare yourself to communicate effectively.

In some cases, this might mean you need a mediator. Be careful when selecting mediators and arbitrators – make certain they are impartial to both of you. Lopsided support only exacerbates communication problems. Never involve either of your parents or your children. Communication between a couple must remain strictly between that couple, with the only help being a qualified marriage counselor.

More extreme situations might call for seeing a suitable psychologist or psychiatrist. If there are *any* trauma or addiction issues affecting either of you, you need to seek qualified and suitable professional help. Certain types of trauma and all types of addiction create unpredictable behavior, even after treatment. If this is the case in your situation, it is advisable to maintain separate accounts and/or perhaps use legal contracts to protect your interests. Unpredictable behavior is unpredictable. A recovered addict is as unpredictable as a practicing addict. Don't be in denial about this fact. When you face the reality of who you are dealing with, you will better maintain the relationship without jeopardizing your own financial interests.

You can predict that unpredictable people will always be unpredictable.

If you are the person with the unpredictable behavior, do something to hold yourself accountable if you want to be fair to your loved ones.

Before you try to communicate with your mate, make a plan. Determine what you need to do to be more effective.

If you are in a good spot with your mate and never really thought there was any communication problem between the two of you, you are in a better spot now:

- By focusing on matters of wealth, you are better able to communicate.
- You now understand a little more about the differences in the way men and women process information, so you might communicate in ways which are more comfortable for you both.

If you are in a bad spot, or even if you are in just a not-the-greatest spot, you have some work to do to create a way in which to communicate effectively with your mate. Chances are if you have *any* work to do in this area, just the thought of talking about money with your mate ruffles your feathers. Before you attempt to communicate with anyone about your wealth make certain your attitude is in check and that your true intentions are to communicate, and not to bash, belittle or badger. When attempting to communicate about something important to you both, it is imperative that you do not bring other issues into the conversation.

Be delicate when initiating dialogue about money with your honey.

No matter what your situation is between you and your mate, opening dialogue about money can be delicate. It is advisable to begin by asking your mate about his thoughts. Perhaps say something like: "I think it would be a good idea if we had a discussion about our overall wealth management plan. What do you think?"

By identifying potential hurdles, you can determine more appropriate ways to approach your mate. Remember it is your responsibility to figure out an effective way to communicate. Getting mad at the same old things about the same old person isn't going to help you or your situation. You need to be open to changing the way you do things if you expect change in others.

Your objective is not to make your point, but rather to create an environment conducive to effective communication. Remember that effective communication requires *two or more* people believing that it *is* effective; not just *one* person, but *everyone* involved.

Keeping in mind gender differences, remember that males prefer short, concise direction. The less you say, the more he will listen.

Gender differences: the less you talk, the more he listens.

While keeping your comfort zones in mind, focus on his comfort zones when you are trying to create a cooperative environment in which to discuss money.

- "Honey, would you have time next Monday after the football game to talk to me about paying off our mortgage?"
- "Would it be possible for us to get together over a beer at the sports bar to talk about the kid's allowances?"

Your money is your responsibility – so learning to effectively communicate with your mate is part of your wealth management responsibilities...not his.

Men want clear instructions.

It is always a good idea to share your concerns and ideas in small doses, and short talks. Begin with less emotional issues and work up to the hard stuff. Once better communication practices have been established between the two of you, then you can tackle the tough stuff.

Even so, ALWAYS keep in mind the gender differences.

He will ALWAYS have a tendency to want get to the point, while you won't.

He will ALWAYS have a tendency to want specifics, while you won't.

You will ALWAYS have a tendency to reach a consensus which FEELS right for some reason you can't explain, while he won't.

You will ALWAYS have a tendency to drag out the conversation into the wee hours of the morning, while he won't.

Men actually want to be told how to please their woman. Remember, males are literal. It is your own natural gender instincts which make you feel uncomfortable having to tell your mate what you want. Remember, women are contextual and hate having to explain in detail what they want.

Women just want their man to know. Well...he doesn't, but he likely wants to, so you need to tell him.

Recall for a moment Deb, whose husband spent all their money giving her a home of her dreams? Her desire was to have a better home – and a retirement fund. His goal was just to make her happy. He didn't care if it took his last dime – which it did. The lack of effective communication nearly cost this couple their marriage, and it certainly cost them both heartache.

If money in the bank gives you a sense of security, then you better make it clear to your spouse that it does. Otherwise he is likely to assume making you happy means something else, like taking you for a boat ride in a new boat, or on a motorcycle ride on a new motorcycle.

Use what you know about gender differences to help you.

- Never sit face-to-face. Always sit side-by-side.
- Allow him to focus on something else while you are discussing money: a ballgame, a newspaper, maybe driving the car.
- Accept his conclusions as soon as he gives them. Don't make him explain it in four different ways. If he says, 'Okay,' then accept it as his final word and stop talking.
- Be concise. Several short conversations over a period of time will be more effective than one long drawn out conversation.

Use what you know about your mate and about yourself.

- Does your mate refuse to discuss money with you because you've never given him a reason to trust your ability to manage wealth?

Maybe you need to clean up your act before you initiate discussions about money. You might even need to ask: "What do I need to do to repair the damage I've done?"

- Does your mate refuse to discuss money with you because he believes it is a man's job to manage the money?

- Why is he reluctant to discuss money?
  - What has been his experience?
  - What has shaped his attitude?

Effective communication does not guarantee you will hear everything you want to hear. Part of effective communication is accepting what you hear. Whatever your mate tells you, respond to is as though it is fact until he tells you otherwise. If you truly believe he doesn't mean what he says, clarify what you think he said and ask him if you understood him correctly. Do not assume he thinks any other way than what he tells you. Remember, men are literal. They say what they mean. The more you know about him, the easier it will be for you to figure out ways in which to more effectively work with him on matters of money.

Effective communication is accepting what you hear.

Smart women don't sit around hoping their toads turn into princes. They preside over their queendoms like the queens they are.

But your queendom includes more people than just your mate, and you need to effectively communicate with all your subjects.

Gender differences enter into professional relationships. Only this time, it is yourself you need to better understand.

When a woman seeks financial advice from a professional, she is more likely to judge the relationship on how she feels, how the advisor makes her feel, and how comfortable she feels in the relationship. This creates vulnerability because salespeople are trained to make people feel like they are making a good decision when they decide to buy whatever the salesperson is selling.

Sales people entice the emotions of others, particularly women.

A male salesperson tends to believe he has the 'right' to make the sale. Remember males have a 'rights-based' mentality.

A female salesperson tends to believe she is 'doing the right thing' by making the sale. Remember females have an 'ethics-based' mentality.

Male customers are as vulnerable to these tactics as females; however, males have a far greater tendency to represent their own interests over anyone else's – again, that rights-based mentality. In comparison, females tend to give more consideration to others – again, that ethics-based mentality. Women have been known to buy things merely to avoid making the salesperson feel bad. It is why home parties are successful marketing tools; women will buy things to please others.

Do you see how females could be more vulnerable to salespeople? Now add in the fact that generally financial advisors are male, and you have another aspect that holds power. Males assume more power over females, and females allow it. Whether it be a socially learned trait or a natural one, it is only important that you realize such traits exist between the genders. You are as affected by them as everyone else, even on professional levels.

I am not saying that you should distrust all financial professionals, nor that you ignore all your natural attitudes and emotions. What I am suggesting is that you acknowledge these basic traits and consider them whenever you interact with others relative to your wealth issues. Be aware that your gender has inclinations which may or may not be in your best interest. Be vigilant about not letting your emotions rule your financial decisions.

This little talk we are having is similar to the little talk your mother had with you about boys long ago. Little has changed in the fact that boys tend to want things from you that you shouldn't be so willing to give. Even so, that shouldn't stop you from creating good relationships with them.

There is a lot more about this subject, and if it is something you believe you ought to look into, my suggestion would be to Google 'gender differences'. The take-away here is to realize that you are different than men. Therefore, anytime you need to communicate with a male for any reason, particularly important ones, you need to understand what those differences are.

Marketing to women is vastly different than marketing to males. Some industries have adapted well and have profited ever since. The financial industry is lagging far behind, however. As women become the holders of a greater portion of wealth in this world, the financial services industry wants to meet their demands, but they just don't know how yet. You need to tell them.

What can you do? I can't give you that answer. All I can do is to encourage you to demand what you need at any given moment. If you need an explanation – demand one. If you need to meet in a more female-friendly atmosphere, such as your favorite restaurant – demand it. If you want to have your friends present to help you absorb information – demand to have them present. If you want to think about something a little longer – demand to do so. If you want anything at all, demand it.

Eventually this will alter the way in which the financial industry delivers products and services to women, but don't plan on that happening anytime soon...or even in your lifetime. Someone needs to start the ball rolling. Let that someone be you.

Some things which tend to affect women adversely are:

- One-on-one meetings. Being alone with a professional causes women to put up an emotional guard.
- Male attire, suits, ties, starched shirts all send messages of power to which women have a strong tendency to succumb to when worn by a male; but when the person wearing the suit is a woman, females have a tendency to feel competitive. Neither emotion is conducive to helping you make sound decisions. Avoid such distraction, whether it be conscious or subconscious.
- Environments where wood, leather and glass dominate cause women to feel intimidated, exposed or less powerful. This is based on scientific studies. Even if you love all these elements, it might just be because these elements evoke such a response

which you subconsciously view as desirable. Put these things elsewhere in your life where they won't interfere with the decision-making process regarding your wealth.

- Scents, such as tobacco, wood, leather, or spice causes women to feel vulnerable. Even a lack of calming scents has a similar effect. Again, become cognizant of how these elements affect your decisions.

- Illustrations or artifacts of violence or speed, cause hormonal disruptions: Guns, motorcycles, cars, boats, etc. Again, while these things may excite you, know that they do little to put you in the right frame of mind to make important decisions.

Elements which tend to empower females:

- Groups, particularly groups of other like-minded women. There is safety in groups. Seminars, courses, and other events which center around financial matters are more appealing to women.

- Fragrances and scents which are food-based or flower-based have a calming effect on women. Bring your own essential oils or put a dab on your sleeve before you go to a meeting with your financial advisor.

- Soft fabric and harmonious colors and patterns make women feel safe. Notice which environment you are in and listen to your emotions closely.

- Pictures of children, pets and other women have a calming effect on women. Photographs of cars and motorcycles do not - whether or not women find the subject matter interesting. Model airplanes, model cars, guns and other male-oriented memorabilia does not put a woman at ease. If your advisor has a lot of this in his or her office, suggest you meet in the office conference room instead.

- Pictures, illustration and color are acceptable educational tools for women. Market and portfolio reports which are all text, or use percentages for comparisons, and/or reports which lack illustrations, color, or pictures have a negative impact on most women. Ask for illustrations and graphs. There is nothing embarrassing about not wanting to read reports. You have every right to ask for something more pleasant, and to some degree this is the only area in which the financial industry has begun to favor you. They are providing illustrations more these days than ever before. So keep encouraging that by asking for more.

To thine own self be true. This is not a time to buck up and take it like a woman. That's what we've been doing for decades. It is time to act like the woman you are and demand that the world of finance adjust to you. Just like men need to be told exactly what to do to keep you happy, so does the entire financial world. Remember it was created by and for men, and still is dominated by men. So, you need to treat it like a man – ask for what you need.

CHAPTER 16:
You can do it!

It is time to apply what you've learned using a new method which incorporates shopping for advice, rather than being sold on any one particular product or service.

While you never need to become an expert, you need to have a basic understanding of each of the five areas of finance and how they affect your wealth. If we were to rate each area of finance according to their importance to your money it would look like this:

1. **Taxes:** Taxes impact your financial situation more than anything else – whether it is the more or less you pay in taxes, or the more or less deductions you claim on your tax return, or the ratio of what you pay in taxes relative to the benefits you receive from your government: safe environments to work and play, legal systems to protect your interests, food and drug regulation, laws, and entitlements such as Medicare and Social Security benefits – among many other things. Tax incentives and tax shelters should be the first place you look to maximize your wealth. Vote according to <u>your</u> financial situation. Politics is all about economics, which affect you regardless of whether you realize it, so realize how each political platform or candidate will actually affect you and vote accordingly. Our system of government was created to serve the needs of the majority.

Women are the majority. Identify your needs and make them known so our government system can do its job.

2. **Insurance:** Protect yourself. You are a money-making machine. You need to protect yourself and others should it ever break down or die. Your earning potential is your greatest resource. Protect it.

3. **Law:** Law is your greatest power, or it can be the biggest noose around your neck. Either way, no one escapes the law. You either use it to your advantage, or it will be used against you for someone else's advantage.

4. **Banking:** Bank products and services is like the handy little tool chest you keep upstairs for simple repairs. Learning to use some of the tools of banking will enhance your financial opportunities.

5. **Investments:** Finally we come to the thing that most people think is the most important aspect to wealth management – certainly it is what the investment banks want you to think – but actually investing is the least important aspect to sound wealth management. Although investing offers you the greatest opportunities to keep pace with inflation and to grow your wealth over long periods of time, it is also the single most influential aspect to wealth management that causes the greatest financial losses. Never invest anything you cannot afford to lose.

The process to wealth management is FIVE steps:

1. **Write down your goals.** Know what you want and when you want it. Write it out in a statement that clarifies your particular concern or desire. Be sure to write it down on paper.
2. **Shop for advice.** Go to qualified financial professionals in all five areas of finance. Present your written concern or goal to a banker, an insurance agent, an investment advisor, a Certified Public Accountant, and an estate or elder law attorney. DO NOT BUY ANY PRODUCT OR SERVICE AT THIS TIME. Take notes as to what each tells you. Find out the cost, complexity, and availability of all the products and services conveyed. You are just shopping at this time, NOT buying.

3. **Carefully consider**. In the safety of your home, carefully consider and compare all your options using the notes you took when you met with various financial experts. Consider the benefits and the drawbacks of each potential solution before you make a decision. Be cognizant of the cost.

4. **Buy.** Once you make your decision, buy the product or service you've chosen. Do not delay in completing this step, as things change more quickly than you might realize. Treat professionals with respect, but maintain control.

5. **Revaluate**. At least once a year, reconsider your choices. If something needs to change, follow the same exact process to determine a new decision.

If you follow these steps verbatim, you will effectively manage your wealth in all circumstances throughout the rest of your life. While this method may seem like a lot of work, after a few visits with each type of advisor about your specific goals you will become better informed about how each area of finance can help you specifically. Then, just a phone call to each now and again will provide you with the information you need to base all future decisions. This method actually eliminates the need for you to inundate yourself with too much information. This method is the most efficient and effective way to properly manage wealth.

You are not alone if you wish managing wealth didn't take so much effort, but because you already put forth considerable effort to acquire your wealth, does it not make sense to put a little more energy into learning to manage it in way that will maximize the value it offers you?

Besides, there are no better alternatives. You only have the following choices:

1. You can hope and pray that you will be the lucky one whose dreams will all come true without ever lifting a finger to do anything to help yourself, but that would be foolish, or

2. You can study all the ways to manage money from all the books on the subject until you understand all the options for every given

situation, and feel competent to apply your knowledge, but that would take decades, or

3. You can trust a salesperson to tell you what you ought to do with your wealth, like you and everyone else has been doing, or

4. You can use this method which allows you to maintain total control of your wealth while using the expertise of others.

Your money is a primary resource for making your dreams come true. You are the one in charge of your life. All the money which you currently have in your possession, combined with all the funds destined for you, is yours to manage. What you do with your money, including co-mingling it with someone else's, is your choice. If you put it toward your goals or allow others to pillage for their own purposes, either way, it is always your choice. Your choices either construct conduits through which your resources are channeled toward achieving your goals, or they destroy these channels which reduce your chances of living your dreams.

Your choices either promote the fulfillment of your dreams or prevent them from happening.

Live the life you were meant to live. Use your money as a resource to provide you with the items and experiences you need to fulfill your deepest desires. That said, while you go gallivanting on your great adventure, bring along your brain. Make certain you have the essentials in life: shelter, safety and sustenance.

You are born with all the abilities one needs to manage their wealth, and as a woman you even have a few extra attributes working in your favor. Now you understand there is more to managing wealth than just investing it, and how important it is to coordinate all types of advice from all types of professional advisors. You are the *only* person who *should* make any decision about your wealth. You are ready and able to take control of your future.

You now know everything you need to know to manage your wealth more effectively than anyone else in the world. You don't need to be an expert at anything. The only thing you need to be an expert on is yourself. Know what you want and use your wealth to obtain everything you need to live the life you were meant to live.

Live your life fully and completely.

Your opinion is valuable. Please write a review of this book at
www.amazon.com and www.barnesandnoble.com
so others may benefit.

SOURCES

The following sources were used to form the opinions in this book and to support relative facts conveyed in this text.

- The Economist, Daily Chart, Women's Wealth is Rising, March 2018
- NextShark, June 17, 2016, Women Now Control 1/3 of the World's Wealth
- Forbes, 2016.06.16, Women Hold Nearly One Third of Global Private Wealth
- 2016 Bureau of Labor and Statistics
- 2008 Bureau of Labor and Statistics
- Business and Professional Women USA, 2003: 101 Facts on the Status of Working Women
- Boston Consulting Group, file 31680, Women Want more in financial Services
- Time Magazine, June 7, 2016, Women's Wealth Growing Faster Than Men's
- Gender-Lens Wealth – UBS, March 6, 2017
- Global Wealth 2016: Navigating the New Client, June 3, 2016
- Financial Post, business, June 16, 2017, 1% of Population Set to Control Half the World's Wealth by 2021
- Piketty.pse.ens.fr>BCG2011, Global Wealth 2011: Shaping a New Tomorrow
- www.money.cnn.com/2017/03/08/investing/vanguard-jack-bogel-stock-market-not-in-bubble/index.html?iid=hp-stock-com, 2017: The Year of Financial Feminism
- https://faculty.haas.berkley.edu/odean/papers/gender/goyswillbeyboys.pdf
- http://money.cnn.com/2016/12/30/investing/stock-market-2016-women-beat-men/?iid=el
- Neilsen, Insights, 2013, U. S. Women Control The Purse Strings
- Institute for the Study of Secularism in Society and Culture, Trinity College, Hartford, CT
- The Family Caregiver Alliance
- Social Security Office of Policy, article by Purvi Sevak, David R. Weir, and Robert J. Willis, Social Security Bulletin, Vol. 65, No. 3/2003/2004
- Transamerica Center for Retirement Studies
- Employee Benefits Research Institute
- Warren Buffett Invests like a Girl, by LouAnn DiCosmo, TMG Bling, March 20, 2008
- Intelligence In Men And Women Is A Gray And White Matter, ScienceDaily, Jan. 22, 2005
- http://www.businessinsider.com/author/ryan-gorman: Women Now Control More Than Half of US Personal Wealth, which will only increase in years to come, 2015
- https://www.capitalgroup.com/our-company/news-room/women-investors-buck-stereotypes.htm
- www.fidelity.com/about-difelity/individual-investing/better-investor-men-or-women
- https://investmentinstitute.wf.com/women-investing
- Boston Consulting Group, publication, Global Wealth 2017: Transforming the Client Experience, June 13. 2017
- Boston Consulting Group, Global Wealth 2016: Navigating the New Client Landscape, June 15, 2016

- http://piketty.pse.ens.fr/files, BCG2011.pdf, Shaping A New Tomorrow, 2011
- The Female Investor: A Cautious Search for Surefire Bets, February, 25, 1995
- From the Age of Aquarius to the Age of Responsibility, report by the Pew Research Center, December 2005
- Philosophyofbrains.com, Do Women Have Different Philosophical Intuitions than Men? Eddy Nahmias, July 15, 2013, Academia / Climate for Women
- Wesley Buckwater and Stephen Stich, 2010, the hypothesis of differences in intuition between men and women
- Daily Mail, uk, Dec. 4, 2013: Men's and Women's Brains: The Truth!
- Philosophyofbrains.com, Do Women Have Different Philosophical Intuitions Than Men?
- Cornell University, Feb 1, 2013: Death of Paradox: The Killer Logic Beneath the Standards of Proof
- Sharing the Wealth: Female Philanthropists Open Up, Helen LaKelly Hunt, March 28, 2007, Women's enews
- Courting Female Philanthropists Makes Good Financial Sense, Anne M. Connor, Fundraising forum, May-June 2002
- American Institute of Philanthropy
- Bank of Montreal's Wealth Institute library
- Male and Female Brains, Summary of Lecture for Women's Forum West Annual Meeting, San Francisco, California 2003
- Journal of Financial Planning, March 2007
- Business and Professional Women's Foundation, 2004 research by Dr. Vicky Lovell and Tori Key, Institute for Women's Policy Research, Working women Speak Out
- Gender and Economic Security in Retirement, U.S. Bureau of Statistics
- Infoplease Almanacs: Median Annual Income, by Level of Education, 1990-2004
- Women's eNews website archives
- Center for Retirement Research at Boston College, November 2004 study
- Center for Women's Business /research 2004, 1998
- U. S. Internal Revenue Service, Statistics of Income Bulletin, Winter 2005-2006, Volume 25, No. 3
- https://womensvoicesforchange.org/financial-knowledge-empowerment.htm#comments
- U.S. Demographic Reports, Census Data from 2000, 2007, 2012 projections
- Business and Professional Women's Research Library
- Institute for Women's Policy Research analysis of the 2003 Annual Demographic Supplement to the Current Population Survey
- National Center for Health Statistics, 2003
- https://insights.som.yale.edu/insights/can-you-get-higher-returns-from-low-risk-stocks
- Pew Research Center, 2005
- Women's Institute for a Secure Retirement, The Female Factor, September 2005
- Americans for a Secure Retirement, September 2005
- Oppenheimer Funds Survey, 2006 Women & Investing Survey
- National Center for health Statistics, 2003
- U.S. Bureau of Labor Statistics, April 2003,, May 2004

- U. S. Census Bureau, 2000
- U. S. Census Bureau, 2010
- www.ned.upenn.edu/apps/faculty/index.php/g275/p1938061
- Health Insurance Coverage in America, 2002, Catherine Hoffman and Marie Wang
- Employment Characteristics of Families in 2003, U.S. Bureau of Labor Statistics, 2004
- Journey to Work, 2000, by Clara Reschovsky
- Wharton University of Pennsylvania, Executive Education Case Study: Institute for Private Investors
- 1990 data, Barry A. Kosmin and Seymour P. Lachman, "One Nation Under God: Religion in Contemporary American Society"
- Change in Big 10 States, Minnesota State Economist, Tom Stinson and Minnesota State Demographer, Tom Gillaspy, September 2005
- Hall Booth Smith, Feb. 9, 2017: The Use of Revocable or Living Trusts in Your Estate Plan
- Estate.findlaw.com: Why Setting UP a Living Trust May Be Unnecessary
- www.peopleslawyer.net: Living Trust scams and the Senior Consumer
- www.tn-elderlaw.com,resources, Timothy L. Takacs, Certified Elder Law Attorney: What No One Tells You About Living Trusts

About the Author:

Susan Joyce is an award-winning financial advisor, a lecturer who has facilitated hundreds of presentations and seminars in the area of financial management, business development and marketing, career and personal development, and economic trends and political impacts on personal finance. She has served various local, state and national organizations to promote women's rights, is listed in the Cambridge Who's Who Registry of Executives and Professionals, serves as an advisor on academic boards and finance committees within her community, founded and directs the Women's Financial Focus Groups of Minnesota and continues to work passionately to educate people, particularly women, about the world of finance for the purpose of empowering them to live their lives fully and with greater purpose.

Financial Security
Once and **For All** and **Forever**
How *Real* Women Manage Wealth

The following articles support the topics found in this book in more detail and are available for purchase at:

www.RealWomenManageWealth.com

Article # 1 How Real Women Get What They Want
Identify what you really want out of life.

Article # 2 How Real Women Adapt Gender Differences
Recognize the power and limitations of being a woman.

Article # 3 How Real Women Guard Against Sales Tactics
Protect yourself from people capitalizing on your vulnerabilities.

Article # 4 How Real Women Vote
Understand the impact government has on your personal wealth.

Article # 5 How Real Women Treat Tax Laws
Maximize tax advantages for every stage of life.

Article # 6 How Real Women Utilize Bank Products
Fully utilize bank products and services.

Article # 7 How Real Women Buy Insurance
Effectively use insurance products as a wealth management tools.

Article # 8 How Real Women Shop for Investment Advice
Get what you need without giving them more than you should.

Article # 9 How Real Women Lay Down Their Own Law
Incorporate legal services efficiently and effectively.

Article # 10 How Real Women Change the World of Finance
Demand what you need from the financial industry.

Coming Soon!

The Wall Street Series Novels, by Susan Joyce

When folks from Main Street wind up on Wall Street anything can happen and does. The series tackles environmental issues, economic inequality, domestic abuse, and justice from the perspective of the common ordinary person. With a twist of humor and characters you will want as your friends for life, this series reveals the confounding way in which humanity ignores its own truths and winds up doing good anyway. Capturing the frenzy of Wall Street, these stories reek of homespun sentiment. They will make you laugh, cry and wonder whether you are laughing or crying over anyone but yourself.

Rigged (scheduled for publication Spring of 2019)

A young ecologist struggles against male-supremacy in her attempt to save the world and unknowingly sets off a series of events on Wall Street which actually could.

Rooked (scheduled for publication fall of 2019)

A young man who found fortune on Wall Street must make a life and death decision whether to accept his fate, or become another Wall Street god during the days leading up to the Global Financial Collapse.

Redeemed (scheduled for publication 2020)

An abused woman rises to protect her children from an awful fate and to maintain custody as she legally battles an evil mother-in-law by utilizing the opportunities she creates for herself on Wall Street.

Find links to these books when they become available at:
www.RealWomenManageWealth.com

.

Made in the USA
Columbia, SC
16 April 2018